Unity

Unity

Behold How Good and How Pleasant
Ministries from Psalm 133

Lance Lambert

LANCE LAMBERT MINISTRIES

Richmond, Virginia, USA

ISBN: 978-1-68389-115-4

www.lancelambert.org

Contents

Introduction

This book has been compiled from ministries of Lance's in 1978 at Halford House in Richmond, Surrey, England. This special message on the topic of unity is as timely and relevant today as it was then. May we hear what the Lord has to say to the churches!

1.
Brethren Dwelling in Unity

Psalm 133

Behold, how good and how
pleasant it is for brethren to
dwell together in unity!
It is like the precious oil upon
the head,
That ran down upon the beard,
Even Aaron's beard;

That came down upon the skirt
of his garments;
Like the dew of Hermon,
That cometh down upon the
mountains of Zion:
For there the Lord commanded
the blessing, Even life for
evermore.

Psalm 133 is a small Psalm, one of the shortest in fact in the whole
Psalter. You can see that it consists of just three verses and we
shall consider some of the lessons of this remarkable Psalm.
(Everyone ought to be able to memorise this little Psalm as we
look at it in these times of study.) Even though it is a short Psalm,
that fact bears no relationship whatsoever to its importance.
This little Psalm is of tremendous importance. It expresses
essential and vital truth. It is the understanding of what the Holy

Spirit is saying in this little Psalm that will be of tremendous blessing and value to all of us, both in the life of the church here and in the work and service of God.

At a first and superficial reading, as with one or two other remarkable Psalms, one feels that it is rather strange. A person with average intelligence, I imagine, reading this Psalm must feel that a whole number of verses have somehow or other got lost on the way. What has Aaron's beard to do with brothers dwelling together in unity? What on earth has oil running down on somebody's beard, going down to the hem of their garment got to do with brothers dwelling together in unity?

One feels a little bit of sympathy with Dr. Moffatt who rearranged the scriptures entirely according to his own idea. Some of you who have ever seen Moffatt's version will remember how you will read verse 1, then 2, then 17, 3, 35, and then 4. He rearranged it as he felt it was most suitable. He was not bound by any views about the authority and inspiration of Scripture and therefore felt that he could make it more intelligible to what, at that time, was the modern reader. The classic example of course is when he came to the little injunction of the apostle Paul to Timothy to take a little wine for his stomach's sake and his oft sickness. He removed it altogether from the text and in the margin said, "The apostle Paul could not possibly have said this." This reveals what happens when we become so subjective in our approach to the Word of God.

At a superficial reading of this Psalm, one must feel that a number of verses have been lost or are to be found somewhere or other in other Psalms and need to be recaptured and brought back to their original anchorage. However, even if we wonder what "the dew of Hermon coming down on the mountains of Zion" has to do with brethren dwelling together in unity, or what Aaron's beard and "the precious oil upon his head that ran right down to the border of his garment" has to do with it, the fact is this: as always, the Holy Spirit knows exactly what He is doing and has arranged this Psalm precisely as we have it. Once we begin to understand both the fundamental lesson of the Psalm and its illustration and teaching, it becomes not just exciting but a window into the purpose and heart of God.

Now with the Lord's help, I want to take the first and fundamental lesson that underlies the whole of this Psalm. We have it here in verse one: "Behold how good and how pleasant it is for brethren to dwell together in unity." Will you please note this little phrase 'brethren dwelling together in unity'? This word, *in unity* in Hebrew, the word that we get the word *one* from, just means really *unitedness* or *togetherness*. We have a little word in front of it which intensifies it, so that in fact as our version puts it in English, "Behold how good and how pleasant it is for brethren to dwell *together* in unity," the *together* and *in unity* in Hebrew is one word. But it is an intensive feeling, so it is quite right to translate it this way in English. Brethren dwelling in togetherness. Brethren dwelling in oneness. That is what this Psalm is all about. This is its basic lesson.

"Dwelling"

Now, I want you to notice that the Psalm speaks of *dwelling* together in oneness. It does not speak of something which is a temporary lodging. It is not a fleeting, transient experience.

It is not some high point in a conference, in some great gathering together of the people of God, where for a few moments, for a few days, we feel the unity of the Spirit. Some point where everything in the garden goes beautifully and we just feel we have been on the mountaintop in an experience of the unity of the Spirit. The Psalm is not speaking about this. It uses a word which is very interesting, "How good and how pleasant it is for brethren to *dwell* together in unity." That is something settled, something stable, something fixed, something established. This dwelling together in Christ means that these brothers have found their home together in Christ. They have found their abode together in Christ. They have found their fixed centre together in Christ.

The word is a wonderful word in Hebrew. It is a word from which we get the word for the Jewish settlement: *Yishuv*—the settlement. It is just this thought of making one's abode in a place, settling in a place, becoming established in a place, getting rooted in a place. There is nothing transient here, no high point of experience, but something which is routine, something which colours the whole of life. Everything takes its colour and its texture from this basic dwelling together.

"Brethren"

Then, another thing before we look a little more at this whole matter in the text. It says, "How good and how pleasant it is for *brethren* to dwell together in unity." (Now you sisters do not have to feel cut out here. The thought is not just brothers, although it is a marvellous thing when men do dwell together in unity and it is an even *more* wonderful thing when women dwell together in unity!) The fact remains that this word covers both. Brothers or sisters, it does not matter. The thought is this: this is not a sentimental unity of *all* God's creatures. It is brethren. Those who have the same parentage, those who have the same birth, those who have the same origin. Those who share the same family name. *These* are those who dwell together in unity.

Now this is very important because years ago no one bothered two hoots about the unity of God's people. Evangelicals were as much to blame as anybody else in this matter and although we believed in some kind of vague mystical unity of the body of Christ, no one bothered about removing the barriers or the middle walls of partitions between us. Of course, the Keswick movement began with that great objective in mind and there were other things too that began a little over a hundred years ago with this great truth in mind. But somehow or other it did not quite bring the final end of breaking down the walls so much that people flowed together. We have to say that it has been the Vatican Council, the Second World Vatican Council, and the impact of the World Council of Churches, which has finally made real believers sit up and have to think again about this whole matter of the oneness of Christ.

Now, there is a danger that we go the other way and include within the unity those who have no business to be in it. It is brethren that dwell together in unity. Those born of God. Those named by heaven with the name of Jesus Christ. Those who have the same origin, born in God's heavenly Jerusalem, God's heavenly Zion. Those are the ones who are to dwell together in unity.

Now that means very simply that if a person, however poor he may be, whatever the colour of his skin, however ignorant he is of basic doctrine, if he is really born of God's Spirit, he belongs to me and I belong to him. If the Lord Jesus has received him, I cannot reject him. If the Lord Jesus has received him, it is incumbent on me not only to receive him, but to find that basis upon which we can dwell together in oneness. This is not to say that we therefore receive every false doctrine and every error and somehow become partakers in other men's sins. (There must be a way through the propagation of error and falsity maliciously and deliberately given.) There are those that in some way or other are just caught up in something because of their background or, so often, it is because of a real desire to find reality, which somehow they do not find in the mainstream institutional denominations. If I find people who are really born of God, that one is my brother, that one is my sister. They belong to me and I belong to them in Christ.

"Good and Pleasant"

Then I want you to notice another thing about this little verse one: "Behold how *good* and how *pleasant* it is for brethren to dwell together in unity." Someone has said that it certainly is both good and pleasant because it is so rare! To find brothers, sisters really dwelling together in oneness is *surely* something that is beyond price. It is good and pleasant. It does not just mean in a kind of nice way that it is good and pleasant, that somehow or other when brethren dwell together in unity the birds twitter and the sunrises and sunsets are the most glorious colours, and everything is beautiful in the picture. Nothing ever goes wrong. No, no, no. But what it does mean is this: when brethren dwell together in unity, the blessing of the Lord is there, the anointing of the Lord is there, the power of the Lord is there, the mind of the Lord is there. It becomes a place of revelation. It becomes a place of expression. It becomes a place of communication. Wherever brethren really dwell together in unity in what the Word of God means by unity, that becomes the means by which the Lord unveils Himself, not only *to* them but *through* them to a dying world around.

Good and pleasant. That means it can be good and pleasant when the whole of hell is allowed somehow or other to destroy that work because of its effectiveness. It is still good and pleasant because the Lord is in the midst. It was good and pleasant in the days of King Hezekiah when he was surrounded by the Assyrian army and that strange gentleman called the Rabshakeh (as Dennis always calls him 'the rib shaker'), stood around the walls and hurled up his insults at those that were within. They were locked up. It was a siege. Nothing could get in and nothing could get out. They were walled up in the city of Jerusalem. Much of the country was occupied by alien forces, powers of darkness, but it was good and pleasant because the brethren within the city dwelt together in unity. They sought the Lord and the Lord spoke to them through the prophet Isaiah. You will remember the great deliverance that came to them.

It was exactly the same with Jehoshaphat when they were surrounded by a whole confederacy of evil and all seemed lost. You will remember the story. Finally, walled up in Jerusalem, they called a fast and sought the Lord. God spoke to them through a prophet and said, "Take your positions, stand still and see the salvation of the Lord." Then you will remember that Jehoshaphat and the other leaders had a little conflab together to decide amongst themselves how could they express their faith in concrete terms. If the Lord had said, 'Take your position, stand still, and see the salvation of the Lord,' how could they express their faith? They did something which many of us have often longed to do. They put the choir in the front of the army as it went out to battle. (I have often thought that would be a way of getting rid of some choirs.) But this choir going in front of them was a very different one. They did not sing some great jingoistic [patriotic] tune about how the Lord is the Lord of hosts and a man of war and He will trample the blood of the enemy under foot and cause it to run all over the place. They sang, really, what was almost like a Sunday School picnic song. One side sang, "the mercy of the Lord endureth forever" and the other side sang, "the mercy of the Lord endureth forever" just as if the enemy was not there. How good and how pleasant it was for brethren to dwell together in unity.

Now we make a big mistake if we think that the goodness and the pleasantness is because the enemy is not there. The enemy may be very much there. He may be laying siege to the whole work of God. He may be causing a spiritual blockade. However, while those brothers and sisters dwell together in unity, it is good and pleasant because the Lord is in the midst. When the Lord is in the midst, no matter what the enemy does, it must not only fail, but work out the purposes of God. In other words, the Lord can turn the very devices of the enemy and the very plans and counsels of the enemy to actually fulfil His own purpose. How good and how pleasant it is for brethren to dwell together in unity.

Of course, we have this in other things too, but we must understand that the enemy's tactics have always been the same.

Where the people of God are drifting in some abstract, vague way, in a kind of corporate self-delusion that they are doing the work of God and proclaiming the Word of God and being effective, the enemy will leave them to it. Sooner or later they will die on their feet. He does not bother them over much except to give them a little prod now and again and make them a little more weary. But where there are brethren dwelling together in unity, the enemy is ceaselessly at work because he has in some way or another to undo that effective testimony and service. It spells the end of his plans. It spells the end of his keeping captives in captivity. It spells the end of his desire to frustrate the Lord Jesus in the building work of the Church. He has to do it. Therefore, the enemy's tactics have always been centred on this one thing: to divide the people of God, to get us all to be at sixes and sevens. Far from dwelling together in unity, we are dwelling together in faction! We are sort of associated together, but not really together. We meet together, but really it is not spirit meeting spirit or heart meeting heart, but really just a kind of physical presence. If the enemy can bring this about, he has effectively destroyed the value of the testimony in that place.

The Day of Pentecost

"Behold how good and how pleasant it is for brethren to dwell together in unity." Now let us look a little more closely at this whole matter. What really happened on the day of Pentecost? "Well," some will say, "they spoke in tongues and others understood." Yes, that is perfectly true, but in one sense (without being misunderstood I trust) that is a detail. "Well," someone else says, "three-thousand were saved!" Yes, that is very true. That was a consequence, but it is not the real significance of Pentecost. What is the real significance? Someone else says, "They were filled with the Spirit, baptised and anointed with the Holy Ghost." That, I think, is getting much nearer to the significance of the day of Pentecost, but still, we are not at the heart of the matter.

What happened on the day of Pentecost? What happened was this: 120 units of a congregation became 120 members of a body. That is the essential significance of Pentecost. Almost overnight! What man could never achieve by training, by courses, by religiosity, by even learning the Scripture, by any other method, the Holy Spirit achieved by coming within and bringing the whole thing within.

Now if you look at Acts 1–2, you must notice one or two things about these 120. I believe that many, many Christians in this country and elsewhere would be very excited if only the conditions immediately after the ascension of our Lord and before the day of Pentecost existed today. One-hundred and twenty born again believers in an upper room—I think most people would be tremendously excited. Here they were, absolutely one! "Of one accord" the Scripture says. Meeting together in one place, of one accord, no faction, no disharmony, no rivalries (seemingly), no jealousies. One-hundred and twenty born again believers. There was not a single unsaved person masquerading as a believer in their midst. "Oh!" you would say, "There is a pure church. There is a pure church!"

Furthermore, they had pure doctrine. They believed in the virgin birth of the Lord Jesus. They believed in His miraculous ministry. They believed in His atoning death. They believed in His bodily, literal resurrection. They believed in His ascension to glory and His coming back again in the future. These things they believed. They were pure in doctrine. I think most of us would be so excited if we could find some company of believers meeting together of one accord around an open Bible that they believed. They had only the Old Testament at that point, but they believed it from Genesis to Malachi and that is more than many, many believers do. Every word they believed to be inspired by God. Their doctrine was pure. Their conception of the Lord Jesus was pure. Could you ask for anything more? They had had the risen Christ Himself in their midst opening the Scriptures to them. It says, "Then opened He their understanding of the Scriptures." You could not ask for more!

If everything called a chapel or a church in this country was like that, many of us would say, "Revival has come! At last, at last it has come!" Everything that is called by the name *church*, born again believers of one accord really praying. Apart from anything else the fact that they had prayer meetings would be enough for us here. We would say, "Oh! This is just wonderful! People praying and seeking the Lord in prayer with an open Bible, a risen Christ, sound doctrine. What more could you ask?" Yet the Lord Jesus said, "Tarry in Jerusalem until you be clothed with power from on high." Why was He so afraid of them getting out? They knew He was risen from the dead. They now had an understanding of the Scripture. Their minds had been opened. They knew He had ascended to the right hand of God the Father.

The point is this: if they had gone out there, they would have reproduced the kind of churches we have today—congregations of units, where we sit somehow in a kind of isolation. Sometimes in some places you can go in, you have known a person for years who you see there and yet you do not know them. You see them sitting over there. You know that they are a believer. You know God has saved them and yet you do not know them, and they do not know you. There is no sense of belonging.

However, when the day of Pentecost came and the Holy Spirit came upon them and into them, something *extraordinary* happened. You must remember that only weeks before these same apostles were squabbling. Who was the greatest? John and James, who of course were in the same family as the Lord Jesus, thought that it would be a very good idea if they kept the positions of the coming Kingdom as a family business. One of the gospels said they asked about it and the other gospel says their mother was sent. I expect it was both. I expect at one point one of them opened up the possibility and faltered somehow and then they got hold of their mother (who may well have been behind it from the start) and said, "Now, Mother, you go and do the dirty work. You go and ask Him. You're His aunt[1]." (She was the aunt to our Lord, humanly speaking.) "Go and say to Him, 'What about the positions either side of You in the Kingdom? What about John and James?'"

They were always squabbling. There were rivalries. Who is the greatest? Who is going to have the biggest position? Who is going to be on Your right hand and Your left hand in Your coming kingdom when You reign over the whole earth? But on the day of Pentecost the most extraordinary thing happened.

1   See Matthew 27:56, John 19:25, and Mark 15:40 for Salome's relation with Mary.

No more question about who was first or who was last or who was greatest or who should be used. Peter stood up and it says the eleven with him. They all stood up, and Peter preached. Now, we know that they also all spoke–the whole hundred and twenty. But it is interesting that Peter preached the great message, and the others were absolutely behind him as if they were saying, "This is us. These words that are coming out of him–Lord, get them out! Get them out!"

You know there was no question of them saying, *"Him*? He denied the Lord three times! If anyone should have preached the first message ever preached up here representing all us lot, it should have been John. He was the one who first recovered and the purest of us all." But no, not a breath. Something had happened! Now it was no longer a question of ambition, no longer a question of position, no longer a question of status, no longer a question of *my* ministry, *my* work, *my* job. Now it was a question of something that was the ministry of Christ, the word of Christ— of God, the service given to us all. It does not matter which one the Holy Spirit takes hold of, providing the Holy Spirit takes hold of *someone* of us and we get the job done by His grace! They had become a body—120 members.

I don't know whether we could put too much on it, but it is an interesting point that before the Holy Spirit came, they threw lots as to who should fill the place of Judas the traitor. It is an interesting fact that from that day onwards, we have no further record of them ever casting lots again. Ever after that they prayed and found the mind of the Lord. It was not lots that were cast to find out who should go out on that great mission to the Gentiles. It was the Holy Spirit who said, "Separate me Saul and Barnabas." In other words, something had happened. The whole thing had gone onto the inside. It was an organic unity produced by the Spirit of God.

Now when we look at the Bible, one of the most wonderful things about the letters of Paul is that they were not written to tell us about an experience that they must all get into; it was written describing something which *was* their experience. It was a definition of something for their help. Do you understand? Oh, what a difference when we have something held up in front of us that is supposed to be the church or whatever and we are told, "Now build this, get into this, do this." Then all our troubles begin. But how much more wonderful it is when we find ourselves flowing together in the Spirit, belonging to one another in the Lord, where we feel somehow or other something organic, and then it has to be defined: "This is that."

A Living Body

It is interesting that it is described as the body of the Lord Jesus. Something organic. You can never have a living, headless body. It can only be a living body when joined to a living head. In Romans 12:4–5 this is how we read the apostle Paul, some years later describing what has come into being, "For even as we have many members in one body, and all the members have not the same office: so we, who are many, are one body in Christ, and severally members one of another." One body *in* Christ, not just one body *of* Christ; one body *in* Christ and severally members one of another. Something has happened that is not just our names on a membership role. It is not just a matter of being given the right hand of fellowship. Something has happened whereby we have been born into an organic entity. We have been born into something, which we can only describe as a belonging to the Lord and a belonging to one another. How wonderful I think that is! This is exactly what we read about in 1 Corinthians 12:12–20:

For as the body is one, and hath many members, and all the members of the body, being many, are one body; so also is Christ. For in one Spirit were we all baptized into one body, whether Jews or Greeks, whether bond or free; and were all made to drink of one Spirit. For the body is not one member, but many. If the foot shall say, Because I am not the hand, I am not of the body; it is not therefore not of the body. And if the ear shall say, Because I am not the eye, I am not of the body; it is not therefore not of the body. If the whole body were an eye, where were the hearing? If the whole were hearing, where were the smelling? But now hath God set the members each one of them in the body, even as it pleased him. And if they were all one member, where were the body? But now they are many members, but one body.

Union with Christ

Now, this really is what we have in this wonderful little Psalm: "How good and how pleasant it is for brethren to dwell together in unity." They have come into something that is eternal—an eternal unity, an eternal reality, a relationship first and supremely with their Lord and Saviour and then in Him with one another.

No wonder the apostle Paul says in Ephesians 4:3, "give diligence to keep the unity of the Spirit in the bond of peace."

What really is this oneness of Christ? What is the Church? Very simply: it is oneness with Christ. That is to put it in profound simplicity. You can forget all the orders and all the positions and all the titles, elders and deacons, and all the varied ranks, gifts and equipment and everything else and come right down to the core, the heart of the matter. What is the Church? Union with Christ and then out of that, union in Christ with one another. Do you get it?

You see, there are not as many Christs as there are Christians. (That is to put it very crudely). But we get this idea because so often in evangelistic services, we are offered a "personal Christ." Therefore, our concepts govern our behaviour. We begin to get a concept from the day we are born again that somehow or other we have a personal Christ. "I have a tailor-made Christ. I have my *own* Christ." Although, of course, once we think it through we realise it is rubbish. There is only one Christ. There may be *millions* of believers, but there is only one Christ. Every single one of those believers is in that one Christ. Whatever his colour, it does not matter! Whether he is Jewish or Gentile, it does not matter! If he is *in* Christ, he belongs, not only to Christ, but to all the others that are there. Union with Christ.

There is only one Christ and if we are all in the one Christ, the one Christ is in all of us. There is not a Baptist Christ or a Lutheran Christ or a Methodist Christ or a Brethren Christ or an exclusive Christ or anything else. There is only one Christ. We may have labelled Him or tried to trap Him into our persuasion, but in actual fact, there is only one Christ, and we are in the one Christ, and the one Christ is in us.

Now, when we begin to see it like that it makes a tremendous difference to our whole concept. We begin to understand, "What is this amazing union that we have come into? I have been made one with the Lord Jesus and Ron has been made one with the Lord Jesus and Bob has been made one with the Lord Jesus and Henry has been made one with the Lord Jesus." Now if I am one with the Lord Jesus and they are one with the Lord Jesus, what has happened to us? We must have come into a relationship with one another. The Bible says, "He that is joined to the Lord is one spirit." I am joined to the Lord, so His Spirit and my spirit are fused into one. His Spirit and Bob's spirit are fused into one. What has happened to us? It is the unity of the Spirit.

Do you begin to see it? Do you see the abuse that we fall into if we begin to label that, or make it smaller than it is. What a terrible thing we do. Thank God, through the history of the Church, God has been recovering one thing after another over these years. I believe the final thing—though it will never be uniform and never systematised, for if you do that you have a hierarchy reproducing the old mistake all over again—but in the end, if only in a remnant, all over the world this oneness will be expressed. *Names and sects and parties fall, Thou oh Christ art all in all*[2]. That is the end: being brought to a full-grown man at the end of the age to the point where the final expression of God's purpose is to be realised.

---

2 From the Hymn *Christ, from Whom All Blessings Flow*

The Impact of Unity

Now, I say that this has a dynamic impact upon the society around. Whenever you have the Church as the Bible calls the Church, when you really have the Church, when you have people in union with Christ and in union with one another dwelling together in oneness, you have a dynamic impact upon the society around. Why? Because first and foremost the supreme impact is upon the principalities and powers, the world rulers of darkness, the hosts of wicked spirits that lie behind the flesh and blood. We can preach till we are blue in the face and find that in the end nothing happens. We can work our fingers to the bone in organising meetings, activity in this and activity in that and *still* nothing happens. But when you have brethren dwelling together in unity, in union with their risen Head, then there is always a dynamic impact upon the society there.

Impact in Jerusalem and Beyond

Think about what happened in Jerusalem. The whole place was turned upside down. See how the whole anger of the enemy was aroused against them and finally they were expelled by persecution and what happens? Wherever they go the same thing happened throughout Judea and Samaria. Before very long apostles have to go down to see what on earth is happening in Samaria. Then they get some deacons appointed to look after the cash side of things because of the widows. There is a little bit of feeling in the church because for some reason or another, the Hebrew speaking widows and needy are being more favoured than the Greek speaking widows. So, the church prays and seeks the Lord and interestingly enough they appoint seven men, all Greek speaking. That was a lovely thing about the Hebrew speaking folks. They all appointed seven people who were in fact the other side. They said, "Okay, okay, okay. You have the seven from the other side and we will see how it goes this time, whether you discriminate against us." No one did.

It was interesting that some of those people, within a matter of a year or two, had become outstanding evangelists and teachers. Stephen became one of the great teachers of the church. So much for trying to relegate deacons only to some kind of menial duty.

Before very long Phillip had become an evangelist—so remarkable! I wish we had a few around like that. Caught up, leaving great big meetings and vast collections to go off to one man. (He was treasurer of the Queen of Ethiopia, but Phillip did not know that when the Lord caught him up and sent him out to join that chariot, baptising one man.) My word, if we had a few evangelists like that what an impact it would be upon society around! It does not matter where this thing goes. Whether it is Ephesus, or whether in the end it is Rome, it turns everything upside-down.

Now dear friends, what was it that turned everything upside-down? Did they have a very efficient fund-raising program? Did they have, in fact, many other things that were well organised? Did they have great theological seminaries or great Bible colleges? It is not that these things are necessarily wrong, but was this the secret of their impact? No. Was the secret of their impact that they had tremendous committees? Committee after committee? Committee controlling committee and more committees? I mean, as there always is in anything successful? No! What then was the secret of their dynamic impact? Oh, was it numbers? It is an interesting thing that in some places they were very few in number, still they turned the whole place upside down, so what was it? I suggest that it was this matter of brethren dwelling together in unity. It was the presence of the organic body of Christ.

What a wonderful thing the Lord Jesus said to Saul of Tarsus on the road to Damascus, somewhere probably around the Golan Heights or just over on the other side, when He met him midday and the sun was eclipsed by the radiant glory of the risen Messiah. Isn't it interesting that when Saul said, "Sir, who are You?" the risen Messiah said to him, "I am Jesus, whom you are persecuting."

Now the apostle-to-be, the apostle Paul, at that time Saul, the unconverted Saul, could so easily have said, "But I'm not persecuting You. You are dead and gone. I'm persecuting these cranks who are followers of Yours; I'm not persecuting You."

However, you see the seed thought in the revelation of the risen Christ had been planted: what you do to born again people, you do to Christ. He and His are one. So glorious was that union from the day of Pentecost that Jesus could say, "Saul, Saul, why persecutest thou Me?" When Saul went away into the Arabian dessert for those three years, I have often thought it must have been this initial revelation that finally began to dawn upon him in ever greater clarity: the Lord and His own are one. How do we explain this union, this entity, this reality, this being joined to Him? How do we explain it?

As I have sometimes said to you—it is fanciful and speculation— but maybe it was in talking with doctor Luke. Perhaps it was Luke that said to him on one occasion, "You know, I think it is rather like the human body. Head and Body. You know, it can only be alive if it's all *joined* together. The body is an organic thing. *One!*" I do not know how it came, but this I do know that the apostle Paul was the first to really begin to use this term "the church which is His Body, the fullness of Him who fills everything in everyone."

Oh, dear children of God, if we could only see this. Wouldn't it transform our whole conception of the gospel? Wouldn't it give us a kind of a glimpse of the objective of God? Instead of relegating this whole matter of belonging to one another, of being built together as living stones into some kind of fanciful, mythological, fairy-tale world, we would begin to see that this is something that is *real*. It is concrete. We need to be built together. We need in some way to find our relationship to one another and above everything else, we need to *guard* that relationship with our Lord and with one another.

Unity Expressed Spiritually

Let me just say something about the expression of this oneness. What is the expression of this unity? First of all, it is spiritual. In Ephesians 4:2–3, the apostle Paul says by the Spirit of God, "Give diligence to keep the unity of the Spirit in the bond of peace." You cannot keep something you do not have. He did not say, "My dear friends, now give all your strength to *producing* unity. Fight for it! Somehow or other you have got to create this unity. This is the ideal, my dear ones. This is the ideal to which we are driving. Now let every fibre of your muscles, spiritually, be strained to attaining it." No, he did not say that. He said, "Give diligence to *keep* the unity of the Spirit." It is something you are born into spiritually. It is something you are introduced to by new birth. You have been brought there when you were converted. Now do not let erroneous ideas or conceptions destroy that unity or devalue that unity, or belittle that unity. Maintain it in the bond of peace. It is a spiritual unity.

It is interesting that in II Corinthians 13:14 the apostle closes his letter with "the grace of the Lord Jesus Christ and the love of God and the fellowship of the Holy Spirit," or communion with the Holy Spirit, "be with you all." In other words, this is again what we are talking about. It is the unity of the Spirit. Only the Holy Spirit can create a sense of belonging. People have their membership rolls, their church order, their church discipline, and all the rest of it, but it does not make you feel that you belong. It is a spiritual thing, this sense of belonging. You may feel that sometimes you are overlooked or somehow or other you are not treated how you ought to be treated, but at least you feel like a member of a family. You belong. It is an inner thing.

Our Lord Jesus prayed for this in John 17 when He said in those very well-known words, verses 21–23, "that they may all be one; even as thou, Father, art in me, and I in thee, that they also may be in us: that the world may believe that thou didst send me." And there is the impact.

"And the glory which thou hast given me I have given unto them; that they may be one, even as we are one; I in them, and thou in me, that they may be perfected into one; that the world may know that thou didst send me, and lovedst them, even as thou lovedst me."

Here you have two things. First, our Lord prays that we may be one even as the Father is in Him and He is in the Father that we may be in them. Then He prays that they may be perfected into one. In other words, you have the basic thing and then you have the growing up. You have the foundation and then you have the "being fitly framed together, growing together into a holy temple in the Lord." That is where we have all our problems isn't it? But isn't it an amazing thing that the Lord Jesus described this unity as the mystical, infinite, oneness between the Father and the Son.

Now I do not care what anyone says, in my estimation you can never trap that truth in a creed. As much as I respect the Nicene Creed and the Apostles Creed, you can never really finally trap into human words the mysterious, eternal unity between the Father and the Son. It is beyond us. How can a finite human being ever quite understand that? It is beyond us. Yet the Son prays that we may be in Them as the Father was in Him and He was in the Father.

In other words, this unity into which you and I have been introduced, this is a partaking of divine life. This is being brought into a relationship with God in Christ. This is so remarkable that we find ourselves in a divine unity. Not to take away from the person of the Father or the person of the Son or the person of the Holy Spirit, but oh, the glory of this gospel! As the Russian liturgy says, Jesus Christ became man so that man might become part of God.

How wonderful it is! How we have devalued the gospel into making it into a matter of just a decision or something about singing hymns and going to meetings and reading a Bible and saying prayers, all those things which are necessary, but that is not the be-all and end-all of the gospel. The gospel is that you and I, by the grace of God, have been saved, born of the Spirit and brought into a union with Christ and with one another. It is a spiritual union. You cannot organise this unity. You cannot somehow or other put it together. It has got to be a recognition on our part of the essential nature of our unity. Now when we begin to recognise with the eyes of our hearts the essential nature of this unity, we begin to flow together. We cannot do it otherwise. It is a *spiritual* matter.

Unity Expressed by Variety

Then another word about this unity—it has great variety. It is not a drab, dull uniformity. Oh, what we people have done to one another in this matter. We have to 'tow the party line.' We have to all look like one another. We have to dress like one another. We have all got to dress in dark colours or somehow alike, think alike, speak alike, intone alike, and everything is alike. It has become such a habit that you can almost tell what particular group a person belongs to by the way they pray!

I knew a pastor who used to tell me he could tell *any* pastor from another denomination by the way they shook hands. I will not go into the details, but he swore that he could detect without ever being told. I don't know, but what I do know is this: it has always been the habit of man to reduce everybody to a uniformity. This is man's idea so often of unity. We produce great political systems, great ideologies that somehow or other trap men and women within them. We have got to make them look alike, act alike, think alike, live alike—everything has got to be the same.

It is not so with this unity. This unity has tremendous variety. I think of the words in 1 Corinthians 12:4–6 where we are told: "There are diversities of gifts, but the same Spirit. And there are diversities of administrations but the same Lord. And there are diversities of workings, but the same God, who worketh all things in all." Followed of course, from verse 14 onwards, "for the body is not one member, but many."

Now when we look through it all, we find that there is a marvellous difference here. One of the lovely things about seeing that our oneness is Christ is that we can all relax! When we see that our oneness is a matter of particular details of doctrine, well, we may all have to tow a party line, or look alike, or act alike, or behave alike, or speak alike. But when we see that our essential unity is that the same Lord is ours, the same Saviour is ours, we are in the same Christ and He is in us, we can relax and be ourselves. If you are a volatile person, you can remain volatile. If you feel like clapping your hands, well okay, you can do so. But we don't look at somebody else and say, "Why doesn't he clap his hands? I must pray for his release." Or someone raises their hands, and we think, "Oh, God do something in So-and-So; they are such exhibitionists. May they be delivered from having to raise their hands." But if someone wants to raise their hands, why shouldn't they raise their hands?

You see, we in this country have always felt that the British temperament, basically phlegmatic and placid and solid, is the temperament of heaven. It is the divine temperament, so that when the Lord gets hold of His Latin or Oriental subjects He will iron them out in time until they take on the British temperament.

When you go to a Spanish meeting, you have hardly bowed your head before someone jumps up behind you and says, "Hallelujah!" and pours out their heart and their soul in a torrent to the Lord. Oh, how lovely! The Lord must say, "I love My Latin people. I mean, if they were all British, think how dull it would be. I love them. They are so solid, they are so unflappable. But oh, I'm glad I've got my Latin people."

I saw a lovely thing in the Garden Tomb a while ago. (I know some of you might possibly misunderstand me, but I thought it was one of the loveliest things I have seen in years.) A group came in at nine-o-clock in the morning to the Garden Tomb, half of them from the West Indies. They sang their hearts out! The other half were very "so-called" respectable, as far as I could make out, from somewhere down south in the States. (Not that I am saying that those from the West Indies were not respectable; they sang their hearts out.) A brother named David was giving a word about the Garden and there was one dear old lady who could not contain herself. I suppose it was her only visit to Jerusalem and her only visit to the Garden Tomb. Suddenly she threw her notebook up into the air with a, "Woohoo!" and it went right up. Then she took her handbag and *whoosh!* It went up in the air and she must have had some Hebron glass in it because it came down with a *crash* on the ground! Then this lady of about 60 did two somersaults and ended with her legs waving in the air! The whole group was shocked! She recovered, sat down, and every time David said "Jesus" she just waved her hand and smiled from ear to ear, with tears running down her face. I thought the Lord must have said, "Oh, how lovely!"

Now, if the British did that, I am sure the Lord would be shocked. He would say, "Goodness! What are they doing?! So unnatural!" But do you see? There was something so beautiful about it. She had met the Lord and she just could not contain herself and she had to express her feelings.

Now of course, in our more ordered meetings we do not like any kind of disturbance. Nevertheless, in this oneness of Christ there is great variety. There are people who are volatile; there are people who are placid. There are people who are cautious; there are people who are always in the front of everything, pushing, straining at the leash to get on and get things done. Our whole job is to stay together, dwelling together in unity. We balance one another, without destroying one another. The person who is volatile does not become vulgar and crude, but somehow or other becomes the enlivening of a whole company of people. Those that are placid and cautious, do not just become that awful, heavy dark hand upon everything, but they become the means of stopping things going overboard into excess and extremes ... when we stay together! The tragedy is when the volatile all go off in a corner and the placid all remain over here. Then there are no longer the brethren dwelling together in unity and there is no impact. Because however much we like it, the world will never feel at home until everyone is together. Until somehow or other there are all the different temperaments, different ways of looking at things, different backgrounds present, at least in one way. We cannot have everything present, obviously.

You can be yourself when you know that your unity is not how you look or what you say, but the fact that you are born of God and you are in Christ and He is in you. Oh, then you can have your Matthews and Marks and Lukes and Johns all expressing Christ, but a different aspect. Put them together and you have the fullness of Christ. Departmentalise them and you only have one-quarter of Christ. How much poorer we would be if we had only Matthew and no John. How much poorer we would be if we had a Mark and a Matthew and no Luke. It is when you have each one expressing his experience and knowledge of Christ that you have the full Christ.

When I was first saved I could never understand why we have Matthew, Mark, Luke, and John. Having never read the Bible till I was twelve years of age, I remember going to a "divine" in the church in which I was and saying, "I can't understand this Matthew, Mark, Luke, and John all telling the same story four times."

He looked at me a bit queerly. I was only twelve or thirteen so he said to me, "Well, sit down, and I'll try to explain it to you. You see, Matthew is Christ as king, Mark is Christ as servant, Luke is Christ as man, and John is Christ as God." He said, "Of course, you see Matthew with his kind of background was very suited to revealing Christ as king. Mark, was the voice of Peter and the hand of Mark. Peter was a fisherman, so he was greatly suited to speak of Christ as servant of the Lord. Luke was a doctor. Who better to speak of Christ as man?

John was the one who was nearest to Him and saw most deeply. He revealed Him as God."

However, I could not understand it then, and in my crass, sort-of arrogant way I said to him, "Well, if I had been God, I would not have done that. I would have taken John, you say he is the most spiritual, and written a four-fold gospel through John—Christ as King, Christ as Servant, Christ as Man, Christ as God—by John the apostle."

He looked at me very sadly, and he said, "Well, one day, if you have the fear of the Lord, you may understand." It was left like that for quite a few years. Then after years I did understand. I understood something. I suddenly realised, this thing isn't automatic. It is not just mechanical. You have to have a Matthew for what he can reveal because of his background, his temperament, his upbringing, everything. When he finds the Lord he reveals the Lord in a certain way. You have to have a Mark who, because of his whole background, and upbringing, and temperament, reveals Christ in another way. John another way, and Luke another way. It is wonderful! Split it up and you only have a little of Christ.

Christians say, "I have everything! I have the whole of Christ." No Christian can have the whole of Christ. Of course, we have the whole of Christ but I cannot contain the whole of Christ. I can only contain a little part of Christ. But when the little part of Christ that is in me, is put in next to the little bit of Christ that is in Ron, we have a fuller Christ. When we add Doug in, we have got an even fuller Christ! When we add Bob in, we have an even fuller Christ! We begin to have a much fuller Christ because, you see, each one of us has only a certain capacity. I cannot reveal all. I can only reveal a little.

That is why, dear ones, it comes down sometimes to interpretation of great truth. You may know that by persuasion, theologically, I am a Calvinist. But there are others here who are certainly not. Well, I don't go behind the scenes saying, "Oh, Lord, the damage So-and-So is doing! Deliver us from this fearful Arminian teaching." No, I understand as Dr. F.B. Meyer once said that one page of the Bible is Arminian, and the next one is Calvinist. I mean, really, it is opposite ends of one pole of truth. However, I cannot get the whole thing in me; I can only get part.

I have perhaps told some of you this story, but just let me tell you it again. Now, I believe people get saved at Billy Graham crusades. The gospel is preached, the challenge is given, someone goes forward, they receive counsel, they sign a card, and they are truly saved! Naturally they think, "Well, I was challenged. I decided for the Lord, and thank the Lord, He saved me!" But what do you do with the friend of mine who was a captain in the merchant navy, a blaggard. I knew both him and his wife. They were an old couple when I was first saved, but I knew, I heard it from their own lips. He was a blaggard and used to come back drunk often. Then he came back this time, drunk, fell in through the front door, managed to get into the lounge, fell flat on his back in the lounge, and stayed there the whole night. He woke up the next morning with a hangover—converted.

How do you explain that? His wife, of course, did not believe in his conversion. She thought that the drink was burning away the vitals, not only of his stomach, but of his brain. Therefore, she felt that she must wait awhile. But an extraordinary change came over him. He no longer swore. He wanted to find a Bible. He spent quite a time searching through everything to find a Bible until he found it and started reading it. He said to me, "I never wanted the Lord." Now, are you going to tell me he is going to be an Arminian? Of course not. What else can he be? He has to be a Calvinist.

But even more remarkable, his wife, sweeping the corridor one day, leant on top of the broom, wondering what had ever happened to her husband, and got sovereignly converted, leaning on top of the broomstick. So, both of them were thoroughly Calvinistic, not in a bad way, but they could be no other.

Now, some people are so small in their whole concept, so narrow in their outlook, they cannot contain that kind of thing. It muddles them, it confuses them, it sends them in a twirl. They say, "Well, there must be something wrong with God." But the fact of the matter is this: that God is bigger than us all.

All I know is there is such a thing as human responsibility and we are called upon by the Lord to make decisions and we are accountable. But I also know that in some strange way, God works all things according to the counsel of His own will. How I tie those two things up, I do not bother my sweet little head. All I can do is give what *I* have and that is to know that God somehow laid hold of me. I can only express what the Lord has revealed to me. But I am very happy for someone else to thunder home the fact that people have got to make a decision because that is the other end of the same truth. Now when we stay together, we have the Bible. When we part, we have sects. When two brothers stay together you have fullness; when they part you have less. Now that is what it means, I think, this matter of variety. It means we can be ourselves. We can relax. We can start to just be ourselves and contribute what we have of the Lord.

There is so much more, really, to be said in this matter. But you see, this matter of brethren dwelling together in unity, once we start on it, where do we end? I would like to say something about the local expression of it. That is quite important and something about holding fast the Head. That is another. I would like to say something about the way of dwelling together in unity. Recognising one another in the Lord. Maintaining the unity. Giving diligence, being careful to maintain the unity of the Spirit, building one another up.

Dear friends if you never contribute anything, you can be sure that you are not maintaining the unity of the Spirit. This unity is not just static. We have to build, just like a living thing. It has to be cared for. Every member of the body has his or her part to play. Whether it is prayer, whether it is giving, or whether it is just doing a practical little job.

I would like to say something about love because in the end that is the key to the whole thing, just loving one another. People say, "I've got no time to do it! Mow somebody's lawn? Or put a screw in for someone who is unable to do it?" These are little, silly little things sometimes, but they all come into this whole matter of loving one another.

People say, "I've got no time! I've got no time." But it is an extraordinary thing. Have you ever noticed that when a young man begins to get an interest in a young lady, he suddenly has a great deal of time? Have you ever noticed that? Certainly, people who have never had time before, have got time—time to play with, time to do this because it is love. When there is real love, there is time. There is time to do the things that ought to be done, both the major things and the minor things. Now, we will come back to this matter again later and look at it a little more as the Lord leads us. Shall we pray together?

Oh Father, we just bow together in Thy presence. We ask Thee, Lord, in Thy love and mercy that Thou would write these words of this Psalm 133 indelibly upon our hearts. We want to be a people who dwell together in unity. We know Lord, we cannot do it of ourselves, but we do praise Thee, Lord, that we have been born into that oneness by Thy Spirit. Oh, Lord we want to be given the power to maintain the unity of Thy Spirit. Help us, Lord, to see the nature of it. Help us to see our part in it and help every one of us to be a contributing factor in the building up of Thy Body. This we ask with thanksgiving in the Name of our Lord Jesus, Amen.

2.
The Expression
of Unity

Psalm 133

*Behold, how good and how pleasant it is for brethren to dwell together in unity!
It is like the precious oil upon the head,
That ran down upon the beard, Even Aaron's beard;
That came down upon the skirt of his garments;
Like the dew of Hermon,
That cometh down upon the mountains of Zion:
For there the Lord commanded the blessing, Even life for evermore.*

This Psalm, which is such a small Psalm, although it is one of the shortest Psalms in the Psalter, its shortness bears no relationship, whatsoever, to its importance. It contains and expresses tremendous and vital truth. We have begun to look at the first verse, "Behold, how good and how pleasant it is, for brethren to dwell together in unity." We have looked a little bit at the language of this verse, of the Hebrew of this verse.

Then, I was beginning to say something about brethren dwelling together in unity. It does not say that this is to be a passing, transient, fleeting experience of unity, a kind of high point, when we go to a conference, when we go to Keswick, when we go to another big convocation. There we suddenly feel that we have touched unity, the unity of the Spirit; we are touching the oneness of the body of Christ. This does not speak of something like that. It uses the word to dwell. How good and how pleasant it is, for brethren to *dwell* together in unity. I think that is our problem. We can all be one for a few days. We can all be one, especially if we are strangers, gathered together in a conference where we have not known each other before. But to live together in oneness, to be established together in oneness, to be settled together in oneness, to make our abode, as the Hebrew is, to make our abode in this oneness, that is far more difficult for most of us. We have said something about the nature of this unity, the oneness of Christ.

Unity Expressed Spiritually

Now I want to take up the matter of the expression of this unity. You will remember I said it is spiritual. It is not something humanly organised, humanly concocted, humanly created; it is a spiritual unity. It is according to John 17:21–23, the same oneness that exists between the Father and the Son. Into that unity we, by the grace of God, have been brought. That is why this whole matter of the unity of Christ, the oneness of Christ, the unity of the Spirit, the unity of the people of God, is of such vital and tremendous importance.

It is why here, for instance, we refuse to label ourselves with any other label than Halford House. This is the house we meet in. We did not want to call ourselves Baptists or Methodists or Presbyterians or what have you. It is not that we are against what God has done in the past, but it is the fact of labelling ourselves in such a way that we become partners and supporters of division. This we do not want. That is why originally we began to come together so that we might just gather simply as believers, born of the Spirit of God, and placed by God the Father in the one Lord Jesus. It does not matter who we are, what our nationality is. I suppose if we counted everyone, I have no doubt that there must be something like 25–26 nationalities here this morning. There are different races here this morning; there are certainly different temperaments. All the different major temperaments and all their combinations are here this morning. There are different social backgrounds, different working backgrounds, and of course, there are different denominational backgrounds if you ever had one. We have got them all here.

However, our unity does not consist in our being good Britishers, or good white people, or good Gentile stock, or whatever else you like to say. Our unity does not exist in any of these things. Our unity lies precisely in the fact that we have all been placed in the one Christ and the one Christ is living in all of us. This immediately means that this unity is a spiritual unity, it is not something which can be concocted. It is true, we have to be perfected into this oneness That is true. It is also true that we need a real work of the Spirit of God upon our lives and in our lives doing something with us. But the fact remains that we are in an essentially spiritual unity.

Unity Expressed in Variety

Then we also said something about the variety of this unity, which means that once we recognize that we are in Christ, we can be ourselves. We do not have to be uniform; we do not have to all look alike, speak alike, think alike, dress alike, or be anything else alike. We can be ourselves. We each have something to give of the Lord which is quite original. We can relax, as it were, and be ourselves in the Lord. We have said quite a bit about that.

Unity Expressed Locally

Now, I just want to take up another matter on the expression of this unity. It is not only that it has great variety, but it is to be locally expressed.

In 1 Corinthians 1:1–2, we read this: "Paul, called to be an apostle of Jesus Christ through the will of God, and Sosthenes our brother, unto the church of God which is at Corinth, even them that are sanctified in Christ Jesus, called to be saints, with all that call upon the name of our Lord Jesus Christ in every place, their Lord and ours."

There is no distinction made here of the believers, except that they are those who are sanctified in Christ Jesus. The word means "set apart" in Christ Jesus in Corinth. This is the church of God, which is at Corinth, those that have been set apart by the converting grace and power of God, placed in Christ Jesus. Now their unity with all other believers is apparent. "Called to be saints with *all* that call upon the name of our Lord Jesus Christ in every place, their Lord and ours."

Psalm 133 says, "Oh, how good and how pleasant it is for brethren to dwell together in unity." Now, dear friends, there is only really one place that we can dwell in at a time. I mean, you cannot be in China, at the same time as you are here in Britain. It is a geographical impossibility. You are either here or there. The fact remains there are people who get over-spiritual in the sense that they say, "Oh, this unity is a spiritual thing! It is absolutely spiritual!" It is all up there in the clouds. There we are one; down here we can fight like cats and dogs. Up there it is all pure; down here there can be every kind of worldly method and technique used. Up there the church is without spot or blemish; down here every kind of spot and blemish is to be found. It is a kind of dichotomy. We have completely divided between *the* church and the churches on Earth, as if what exists as the churches on Earth bears no relationship to *the* church.

Oneness in the Local Church

Now, it is perfectly true that God is perfecting the eternal church, but that church has to be expressed in time and in place. You see, everything is put to the acid test here by whether we can dwell together in oneness in the locality in which we are living. It is all very well to say, "I believe in the unity of the Holy Spirit. I believe in the holy catholic church," as it says in the creed, not meaning the Roman Catholic Church, but the holy catholic church, that is the holy universal church. That is the oldest statement of belief that has come down to us. This statement has come right down from the beginning.

But what do we mean when we say it? I can say, "Oh, I feel so much love in my heart for the believers in Washington." Of course, I can love the saints in Washington, they are 3000 miles away! Anyone can love people who are 3000 miles away. I do not have to serve them. I never have to go and mow their lawn. I never have to go and put a picture up for somebody. I never have to bake a cake to take in for someone who is in need. I never have to go and help in a family situation. They are 3000 miles away! Anyone can talk about being one with people providing they are a certain number of geographical miles away.

God is not taken in by that kind of talk. God says, "Of course, all of you are one! So, you are one with all those that have gone." As the creed says, I believe in the communion of saints. I believe in the communion of saints. What do we mean, "I believe in the communion of saints"? I mean this: that Paul belongs to me, and I belong to the apostle Paul. Peter, the apostle, belongs to me; I belong to the apostle Peter, and Augustine, or Martin Luther, or Zwlingli, or Calvin, or Whitefield, or the Wesleys, or George Fox, or any of the others. We believe in the communion of saints. They have gone on into the presence of the Lord. There are some that we have actually buried in the name of the Lord Jesus, but we believe in the communion of saints. They are not dead, they are alive!

I shall never forget, some years ago, a great saint in the United States. I happened to be with her when someone went up to her and said, "I remember your dead husband." (Now her dead husband happened to be a rather extraordinary servant of the Lord.) This dear one went up and bubbled all over her and said, "I remember your dead husband." I saw her rise up to nearly all six foot that she was and she said, "Dead? My husband dead? He has never been more alive!" She meant of course he was in the presence of the Lord.

It is perfectly true. But you see, we believe in the unity of the church. We are not some little bit of a piece, a little bit of spiritual debris that comes in the 20th century that bears no relationship to what God did at the very beginning in Jerusalem. We are one church. In the end, when time is over, and the former things have passed away, we shall find that we are part of a tremendous work that God has been doing down through the centuries of time, of this age. How wonderful! But my dear friend, of course, I can say I believe in the communion of saints, if they are up there. What have I got to do with them? Being a good Protestant, I do not pray for them. So, I have nothing to do with them. I can just say I believe in the unity of God's people. God is not taken in by this kind of hogwash. God looks at you and says very simply, "What about that person who is a believer, who is in the same company that you are in and in the same group meeting? What about that person? Do you serve them? Do you love them? Do you care for them? Do you pray for them? Are you concerned for their spiritual increase and their spiritual fruitfulness?" Not, "Are you a busy body in their affairs? Are you always trying to manipulate them? Are you always trying to corner them with various pamphlets and books that will lead them into greater blessing?" No! That is not the way to do it. What the Lord wants to know is have you got a heart of concern for your brothers and sisters or are they anonymous faces? Do you ever bother to find out who they are, what they are, what their background is? Do you ever take up this thought we have had at times that if we would all in our groups only pray for one another, if only we had two or three a day, we would soon begin to develop a concern and an interest in one another?

Unity Exposes Us

Now, this matter of dwelling together is not all a garden of roses. I mean, God has designed it so that there are many thorns in the roses. If you think that God is going to be taken in by bringing all sweet people into the circumference of your life, so that you can move along ... again, God is not taken in by this kind of thing. He knows very well what lies just under your skin. You have only got to get the wrong kind of person to have to work with, the wrong kind of person to have to live with, the wrong kind of person to be in a team with, and all that is bad in you will come out. I have seen people who are naturally noble, naturally sweet, reduced to being irritable, bad tempered, and almost vicious by the way God puts them with somebody who just rubs them up the wrong way at every available turn. You see, God knows what He is doing. All that nobility, all that sweetness is skin deep. While the circumstances are right, the real situation will never ever be exposed. But the whole point of dwelling together in unity is to put us next to people that are quite different from us and we just have to come through or die. Now I know some of you feel like dying at the present time, and maybe that is why the Lord spoke about this, I do not know. But the fact of the matter is, I know of no other matter that reduces us to the place where we feel like giving up, than coming up against one another.

Heaven Recognizes No Divisions

Now, we can all smirk about the United Nations. We can refer to it as "Dis-united Nations". We can say that, of course it has no basis because they do not know the Lord Jesus, and in fact, it is not permitted to use the name of the Lord Jesus in the United Nations. We may all smoke about this thing, point out the weaknesses and say, "Of course, the Lord Jesus is the answer," but when it boils down to the real heart of the matter, are we any better? When we look at the Christian scene, when we see the factions and the divisions—big divisions, institutional divisions, divisions that are very respectable—are we any better?

You know, people find it a sort of highly decent and respectable thing to name a division they belong to. It is not so in heaven. No such things are known in heaven. If you got there and one of the angels asked you at the gate, "What are you?" and you said, "I am a Lutheran," immediately, the angel would say, "Lutheran? We know no Lutherans here."

"You have no Lutherans? Oh, you mean they are in the other place?"

"No," the angel would say. "Do you mean Martin Luther? Oh, Martin Luther, he is here, but we have no Lutherans. We have only got believers here. No Lutherans."

"Wesleyan?"

"We have never heard of them here. We have got the Wesley brothers, and the Wesley mother, and some of the other Wesleys, too; they are all here. (She has got a medal for bringing up the Christian family, Mrs. Wesley.) However, there are no such things as Wesleyans."

Now my point is this. When it really comes down to it, we are as much divided practically and realistically, as is the world. This should not be. One of our problems is that we all think we should have the same temperament, or that we have the ideal kind of temperament we feel is right and we are all going to try and be the same. But that is impossible. The only way you and I could be one is to see that we are in the one Christ and the one Christ is in us. Then we can relax and be ourselves in a right way. Allow the Lord to discipline us and allow the church to discipline us. Then things begin to happen in our lives.

This whole matter of the unity of the Spirit has got to be expressed locally. It has got to be expressed in the place where we are living. That is why we become more and more afraid when people come to us from vast distances. Why do we talk about living within the locality? Why do we talk about living within the limits of this particular borough? Because we feel it to be important. If we start going out, and out, and out, what should we do? Finally, include the whole of London? Then we defeat the objective because what happens is people become "Sunday go-to-meeting" believers. They travelled such a distance; they can only get there on Sunday, and then what happens? You do not have this practical teamwork, this practical having to get down to prayer issues together, this having to work things out together, this having to be together in outreach, and many other problems and difficulties.

The church down here, it is perfectly true, is not perfect. D.L. Moody once said, "You will never find the perfect church," when he asked a man what he was doing, why he had left one particular group and was going to another. The man said,

"I am searching for the perfect church," Moody said, "You will never find the perfect church on earth; when *you* find it, it will no longer be perfect."

The fact of the matter is, we have this idealistic conception that somehow or other the church ought to be perfect. Therefore, all the time we leave this group to go to that group because we say, "This one is better." But that is not the basis. You see, the church down here is always like a builder's yard, like a cutting out room of a tailor, like the kitchen in a big family. It is always where everything is being done; there has got to be a mess. That is why God is building the eternal from the local. It is our relationship to the Lord as Head, our relationship to one another in Him that is put to the test. That is why this whole matter of brethren dwelling together in unity is so vital.

Holding Fast the Head

Now, I would like to say just another point here. It is also a matter of holding fast the head.

Colossians 2:19: And not holding fast the Head, from whom all the body, being supplied and knit together through the joints and bands, increaseth with the increase of God.

Ephesians 4:15, 16a: May grow up in all things into him, who is the head, even Christ; from whom all the body fitly framed and knit together through that which every joint supplieth.

This unity is a matter too of holding fast the Head. We do not, in fact, come through by holding fast to one another. In this way, and we have seen it in the history of the church, whole movements of the Spirit of God have gone off the rails, because they have all tried to hold fast to one another, and somehow get a kind of corporate mind on everything, and slowly they go right off the rails.

The thing to emphasize in this "brethren dwelling together in unity" is that every one of us must hold fast to the Head. Then we act as the guarantor to one another; we act as the security to one another. If things begin to go off, we can say something, and it can be respected. We may not always be right. Often people say, "Oh dear, dear they are afraid of this, they are afraid of that." It is amazing once you get together, how as soon as there is some kind of leadership or authority, immediately, we become so suspicious of everything, to the point where God can never take a new initiative. You know the kind of thing. That is unbelief. But if we can hold fast the Head, the moment the Head says, "Take a new step," we are ready for it. We are together. We act as the security to one another. We pray about it together. We know the Lord's mind and act in oneness over it.

It is a matter of life and light and love, basically. That is why we must hold fast the Head because He is the light, and He is the life, and He is the love. When we hold Him fast, we shall be safe, and we shall grow, we shall find one another. If I hold fast the Lord, surely, I must find you if you are holding fast the Lord. Mustn't I? Of course.

The Process of Dwelling in Unity

Recognize One Another in Him

In this matter of the oneness of Christ, brethren dwelling together in unity, what is the way? There are four very simple things. I will only mention them and just a sentence or two on each. The first is to recognize one another in Him. This is the basis of dwelling together in unity. Now, if I will not recognize you because you happen to not believe in a millennium, we are not going to dwell together. All the time I am irritated by you because you do not believe in a millennium, and I think you are plain dumb and stupid. I think worse, I think you are in darkness. As far as I am concerned, the whole Bible screams from Genesis to Revelation, that there is such a thing as a millennium! That you are dogmatic about this matter that you cannot see there is a millennium anywhere in the Bible upsets me to no end. Therefore, I cannot dwell together with you in unity. Of course, if you are going to be entrenched and I am going to be entrenched, we are going to have troubles. It seems to me that if we are on non-fundamentals, not touching the person of God the Father, the Son, or the Holy Spirit, not touching the authority and inspiration of the Word of God, or of those fundamental essentials of the gospel and of the faith, it seems to me we have to give a freedom to one another.

Romans 15:7 says: "Wherefore receive ye one another, even as Christ also received you, to the glory of God the Father." It says in Romans 14:1, "Him that is weak in faith receive ye, yet not for decision of scruples." I fear that does not make much sense to most people. A modern version says, "investigation of his conscience," which is much better. You see, the trouble is we are always investigating one another's conscience, aren't we? As soon as we meet someone, we want to find out, "Are you baptised? Oh, why aren't you baptised? Don't you see it in the Word?" The poor little soul who has been brought up in a completely different tradition, sputters and mutters for a while. Then we say, "But don't you know that every real believer has to be baptised by immersion?" We are investigating their conscience, giving it a good prod; something is wrong with the person's conscience.

You know, we are very amazing in this way. We give God a few days to do something, and when He doesn't, we say, "It's okay, Lord, we'll make up the lack. If You don't speak to So-and-So about smoking, I will. If You don't speak to So-and-So about their attitude to drink, I will. If You don't speak to So-and-So, about their worldliness, I will. Don't worry. That short skirt, hmm, I'll get onto it. We'll get something done about that and it will be dropped by a few inches by next week, fear not."

The point is, if the Lord doesn't speak to somebody, we will. But normally, if we are a little bit spiritual, we'll wait for a little while. Then, if we are a little spiritual, we will drop a pamphlet or a book or some little hints or give a testimony (quite spontaneously, of course) as to how we were delivered. This does more to destroy the unity of God's people than anything else in the world because a young believer, who has not thought about these things, is suddenly subjected to an investigation of his conscience. "Why doesn't he do this? Why hasn't he woken up to this? Why hasn't he settled this issue? Why is he not walking this way?" We all do it. It is amazing.

You remember that word of the apostle Peter. As soon as the Lord said to him, "Do you love Me? Feed My sheep." Peter said, "Well, what about this man, Lord, John?"

The Lord said, "What is that to thee? Follow thou Me."

But we are all the same. We cannot help it. As soon as the Lord speaks to us, as soon as He deals with us, we turn around to the next person and say, "What about him? If You are going to deal with me, what about So-and-So? You have got the lipstick off me, get it off her." Then our attitude is very simple: "Alright, Lord, I will pray about it." Then we feel So-and-So is so thick, spiritually, that God cannot get anything through. Then it is up to us! We will get it through where God has failed.

Now, we do tremendous damage in this thing. The Bible says that we are to receive one another also as Christ received us to the glory of God the Father. How did Christ receive you? He received you as a sinner saved by grace. If that was the minimum ground upon which we received every other brother or sister, it would transform our fellowship. We would not all the time be wanting to get at them.

Now, let me say something about this. You see, there is a great difference between this and a spiritual concern for somebody's increase in fruitfulness. It is a vastly different thing to be really concerned and to have prayed. There are times when we should speak, but oh how blessed it is when it is under the government of the Spirit. When suddenly someone says something, and instead of the other person blowing up, they are ready. They are prepared by God and it really is the Lord. Oh, that is a very different matter.

However, the damage we have done in this matter of brethren dwelling together in unity is because we will not receive one another as the Lord received us. You know, it has taken the Lord years to get me to recognize simple things. Hasn't it with you? I have found that sometimes I suddenly think, "Oh, my goodness, it has taken me all those years because of my particular temperament." Now, other people have got this issue settled in their lives, but they have weaknesses in other ways which I settled years ago. But I have been holding out on something because I don't see it. The Lord has said, "It is no good talking to him about that; it would finish him off. He is such a strong-willed person. It is best just to go along with him because I love him so much. I will go along with him, but right at the right moment, after so long, I will hit him hard." The Lord always does it. Then what a lovely thing it is when saints come along and pick you up. Ah, that is a very different thing, isn't it? The Lord has given you a real blow, and now the saints come in and minister. Then you wake up on this issue at last and you say, "Ahhh."

Give Diligence to Maintain the Unity

Here is the next thing: give diligence to maintain the unity. We have said quite a bit about that, but it is interesting. Ephesians 4:3 says, "Give diligence [be careful] to keep [or maintain] the unity of the Spirit." This unity does not just remain in a static way. We have to give diligence to maintain it. It is not the big issues that sometimes divide us. It is the little foxes that spoil the vine.

Those little darling, little cuddly foxes, are rather smelly a bit later, but when they are young they are not too bad. They get out into the vines and chew the tender blossoms. They do it, not because they like to eat, it is just because they like the smell evidently. They dive in and out of the vines. You must remember the vines are not strung up as they are in Italy, right up high. They are on the ground in Israel. So, these foxes dance in and out of the vines and do a tremendous amount of damage, just one family of little foxes so sweet, so cuddly. They do not look as if they are very lethal creatures. They do not seem to be too harmful, but they are the things that destroy the vines.

Now that is true in our fellowship so often, isn't it? Because we do not give diligence to maintain the unity of the Spirit, then somehow or other, our fellowship begins to deteriorate, and somehow or other, insinuations come in. We all know what it is when a person has become so fixed in their suspicion of us that there is not a thing we can do. They look at us in a dark way, under a cloud, never a smile, never a civil word, because somehow or other, something has happened, which has made them suspicious of us. They no longer trust; you cannot do anything. If something had been done at the beginning—a word in season, a word of apology, a word of explanation—maybe a whole situation would be settled.

Christian work is riddled with this kind of thing. When I go sometimes to servants of the Lord, there they are in the front line, sometimes two of them, sometimes three of them right in the front line, but somehow or other, they will not talk to each other. Two of them have got a long-standing battle. It goes back to some silly little issue years and years back that was never mentioned, never dealt with, nothing was ever done and now it is almost impossible. Maintain the unity of the Spirit. You can never be too careful about keeping the unity of the Spirit.

Build Up the Body

Then a third thing we find in 1 Corinthians 14:26, in Ephesians 4:16, and in Colossians 2:19. It is building up the body. If you and I are going to be brethren dwelling together in unity, we must make our contribution. We have each one something to give as well as something to receive. No matter what it is, it may only be in simple ways, we can all do it. May God help us in this matter of really building up the body of Christ in our home gatherings, as well as in our major ones. May the Lord help us all to be under the government and direction of the Spirit, to know how to follow the anointing and to give whatever it is, whether it is a testimony, whether it is a hymn, whether it is the exercise of a gift, whatever it is, that we may do it as the Lord empowers and directs.

More than that, there are other ways in which we can build up the body. Some people have practical gifts. They can release others to do things by stepping in and doing a simple, practical job. The law of the Word of God is that those that care for the baggage and those that go out to war shall receive the same reward. Now, this is going to be true in the great giving of rewards at the tribunal of the Lord Jesus Christ for all believers. Those who have had to stay behind and do very simple little things. Sometimes, it is a very simple thing.

For instance, here is a person who is at work and has very little, or no ministry of the Word, nothing like that, but they have a good income. What do they do? They make sure they give at least a percentage of that income to the upkeep of some servant of the Lord somewhere, either here or somewhere else. Do you mean to tell me that the Lord one day, when that other person out there gets their reward, does not reward in exactly the same way the person who all through the years has quietly given of their income to the support of that brother or sister? Oh, not at all. They are partners in it, therefore, they shall have the same reward.

Now in this way, we can come into something so blessed. There are all kinds of practical things we can do. It is part of brethren dwelling together in unity. Strains and pressures come upon some of the brothers and sisters in the work of the Lord simply because people do not think about them. They do not care for them. They do not think about some of the practical needs. Indeed, sometimes there is almost a kind of jealousy: "So-and-So out there, sitting around, looking at lovely views, having an exciting life—nearly being eaten by cannibals—quite exciting. Waited on hand and foot by servants. Lovely. Wouldn't mind that kind of life myself instead of this humdrum thing that I have got here at home." Oh, may God preserve us from devilish propaganda and make us those who really support one another.

Love

The last thing about this "brethren dwelling together in unity" is perhaps the simplest, but it is certainly the most profound, and it is the most powerful of all. It is just simply love. We can never forget the fact that 1 Corinthians 13 comes between the great chapter on the body of the Lord Jesus Christ, chapter 12, the great chapter before that, on the Lord's table and our gathering together, and after that the great chapter on the exercise of gifts. Don't you think that's amazing? Again, some people looking through would say, "How extraordinary is this little poem, it is just like the apostle Paul suddenly fell into a kind of poetic trance and wrote a poem that has very little to do with the other part. I think we can lift it out of this, all this business about gifts and diversities of ministrations, and all the body and eyes and ears and feet and hands and belonging to one another. What has it got to do with this most perfect way, love?" But it has everything to do with it because when you love a person, you care for them, and you find time to serve them.

You know, whenever we say, "I have no time to go and see So-and-So," it is because basically we are saying, "I do not love them enough." Whenever I say, "I have got no time to do this, or to do that," it is very often the case that I am saying I really haven't got love. Now, I am not saying you are not busy. I am not saying that you do not have a lot of pressures upon you. What I am saying is this, as I said before, every time a young man falls for a young lady, suddenly the person who had no time, finds time. He has time to be up late. He has time to walk her home. He has time to do all kinds of things and also the other way around, suddenly the young lady has time she never had before.

So, what is the key? Love. Love has made a way, and so it is with you and me. This matter of love is all important. It comes down sometimes to the simplest things, does it not? I remember in some of the great crises of my own life, it has not been the people who have been great spiritual giants who have been a comfort, but sometimes some of the very simple, ordinary members of the family of God, who just made us a cup of tea at a time when we were under colossal pressure. It meant a lot. Sometimes, it is a little practical thing that someone does, and you suddenly think, well, you are remembered. Someone has thought, someone has gone to the trouble just to say to you, "I am remembering you in the trial through which you are passing."

Love is the key to everything. May God preserve us from falling from our first love. If we have fallen, may He restore us. May He give us a baptism in love that will submerge all our problems. I do not believe that as a company, we are an unloving company. I have known over the years a tremendous amount of care and love if we compare ourselves with many others, but that is not the way. If we look at this and that and the other, and we see these cold institutional things we say, "Oh, what love we have!" But that is not the way, is it? The fact is, we are all busy. We all have commitments. We have many, many duties—family duties, work duties, church duties—many things to do.

Oh, what we need is never to allow ourselves to fall out of love with the Lord because then all these duties are submerged in a sensitivity to Him and to one another. It is when that sensitivity is lost. You cannot cut down on the number of commitments you have got, in one sense, you still have got to do them. But when the tide of love comes in, the barriers that go out are simply submerged. May God help us. If you feel, as I often do, a need of love, may He help us to come to Him and put it as simply as this, "Lord, I feel a need of a baptism of love. I feel a need to be submerged and overwhelmed, immersed in Your love again, so that the duties become somehow gilded, they take on a new light, a radiance shines upon them." Certainly, we all know what it is to be served with love. The person doing it may be quite unconscious, but we all know it, don't we? It is the difference between something which is just a duty and something which is out of love.

Shall we pray?

Father, we have been speaking about this Psalm 133, this first verse, about how pleasant and how good it is for brethren to dwell together in unity. Lord, we all want to dwell in that unity. We do not want it to be some fleeting experience, some high point. We want it to be our routine experience, the basis upon which we live and from which, as it were, we serve. Oh, Father, Thou knowest all the problems we have. These collisions we have of temperament, of outlook because of background, because of different cultures and all the rest of it. Lord, Thou canst give us revelation as to our place in the Lord Jesus, and the place of every other believer here in Him. Lord, above all, You can touch our hearts with Thy love. Thou canst melt us afresh, immerse us afresh Lord, in that love of Thine, that will bring to us all a new sensitivity to Thyself, to the direction of Thy Spirit, and to one another, and to the world, outside. Lord, do this, we pray because we want to be in the experience of Thy word, that when everything else fails, love never fails. This we want as our experience, Lord. We want to have that most perfect way of all, and we ask it in the name of our Lord Jesus. Amen

3.
The Precious Oil Upon the Head

Psalm 133

Behold, how good and how
pleasant it is for brethren to
dwell together in unity!
It is like the precious oil upon
the head,
That ran down upon the beard,
Even Aaron's beard;
That came down upon the skirt
of his garments;
Like the dew of Hermon,
That cometh down upon the
mountains of Zion:
For there the Lord commanded
the blessing, Even life for
evermore.

Exodus 30:22–33

Moreover the Lord spake unto
Moses, saying, Take thou also
unto thee the chief spices: of
flowing myrrh five hundred'
shekels , and of sweet cinnamon
half so much, even two hundred
and fifty, and of sweet calamus
two hundred and fifty, and of
cassia five hundred, after the
shekel of the sanctuary, and of
olive oil a hin. And thou shalt
make it a holy anointing oil, a
perfume compounded after the
art of the perfumer: it shall
be a holy anointing oil. And

thou shalt anoint therewith the tent of meeting, and the ark of the testimony, and the table and all the vessels thereof, and the candlestick and the vessels thereof, and the altar of incense, and the altar of burnt-offering with all the vessels thereof, and the laver and the base thereof. And thou shalt sanctify them, that they may be most holy: whatsoever toucheth them shall be holy. And thou shalt anoint Aaron and his sons, and sanctify them, that they may minister unto me in the priest's office. And thou shalt speak unto the children of Israel, saying, This shall be a holy anointing oil unto me throughout your generations. Upon the flesh of man shall it not be poured, neither shall ye make any like it, according to the composition thereof: it is holy, and it shall be holy unto you. Whosoever compoundeth any like it, or whosoever putteth any of it upon a stranger, he shall be cut off from his people.

We have been looking at Psalm 133, and although it is, as I have said, one of the shortest Psalms in the Psalter, this bears no relation at all to the vital importance of the truth it expresses. This little Psalm contains and expresses essential truth. We have already looked at the fundamental lesson about brethren dwelling together in unity.

Now, this time, I want to go on to the second verse: "It is like the precious oil upon the head that ran down upon the beard, even Aaron's beard that came down upon the skirt of his garments." We are given in this little Psalm, in verses two and three, two illustrations of brethren dwelling together in unity. I am not sure that "illustration" is the best word to use. Perhaps, it would be better to say and would bring us far more directly to the heart of the matter if we said that we are given two keys in verse two and verse three. You will notice both begin, "*It is like* the precious oil upon the head ... *It is like* the dew of Hermon that comes down upon the mountains of Zion." In Hebrew, it is very simply a little word that means "like" or "as." "How good and how pleasant it is for brethren to dwell together in oneness *as* the precious oil upon the head that came down upon the beard, even Aaron's beard, that came down to the skirt of his garments. *As* the dew of Hermon, that cometh down upon the mountains of Zion." Now, will you take your Bible, and I would like you to have a little closer look at the text first, and then we will seek to explain and expound it.

The Precious Oil

First of all is the precious oil. It is, of course, the holy anointing oil. This is a reference to the high priest's anointing. It is not the oil that we read of in Psalm 23, "He anointeth my head with oil," which of course was one of the ways that you sort of made yourself feel better. After a weary day, you anointed your head with oil. Sometimes one's body was anointed with oil. It was a common thing in the ancient world, in the hot countries, to bathe oneself or anoint oneself with oil.

However, this precious oil upon the head is the sacred, holy anointing oil with which the high priest was anointed. That passage in Exodus 30 gives us the description of the constituents of this oil, and also tells us that it may not be used for secular purposes at any time. It must not touch the flesh, it must never be used for secular purposes, and it must never,

ever come upon an unsaved person, in other words, a stranger, someone outside of the covenant people. They may be religious, they may be knowledgeable, they may be very zealous and all the rest of it, but if they are not born of God, if they do not belong to the covenant people, this holy anointing oil was never to touch them. There is a very serious warning contained here in the Word as to what will happen to anybody who uses this sacred oil in a wrong way.

Now, there are three things about this anointing oil that we notice straightway from this passage in Exodus 30. First, it is specific, that is, although it was made after the art of the perfumer, it was for specific use. It was not just an ordinary oil that was used on other occasions for other things. This was a special oil made in a special way. It was specific.

Secondly, it was sanctifying. Anything the oil touched was sanctified, or made holy, or was set apart for God. You will read all the different things that were touched by the holy oil. Nearly everything in the tabernacle was touched by this oil. Even the base of the brazen altar was touched, even all the vessels, the little snuffers, the little pots and pans. All of them were anointed with this oil. Not only was the blood sprinkled on everything, but the oil touched everything. The blood meant that it was redeemed, it was, as it were, cleansed, and the oil meant that it was set apart, made holy. Now that is very important, I think, for our understanding.

The third thing about this holy anointing oil that often escapes people's attention is that it was very fragrant. It was aromatic. In other words, when this oil was poured upon the high priest, the whole tent of meeting would have been filled with the fragrance of it, especially as it was not used sparingly. It was poured, as we have in this Psalm, so that it really ran down his beard onto the garment. If we understand, as we shall see in a moment, that it comes down to the hem of his garment, it really was quite a bit of oil that was used. I suppose the whole place was filled with fragrance.

So, we have three very beautiful things about this holy anointing oil. It was specific. In other words, only those things for which God had a specific purpose were so anointed. Secondly, it made those things holy, set apart for divine use and the divine provision. Thirdly, there was a fragrance about those things that was attractive.

The Significance of the Precious Oil

Of course, immediately, we have to ask ourselves what this anointing signifies. In the Old Testament, the anointing oil was, and is always, a symbol of the Holy Spirit. But beyond that, it has another figurative meaning. It is always to do with service. You will find that wherever you look, whenever the holy anointing oil was used, somehow or other, it was to do with the service of God. It was to do with the realisation of the purpose of God, it was to do with the work of God, it was either to do with the actual furniture, or the material things, or the people that were involved in the house and work of God. It has three meanings, which may help us to understand. We all understand the third, but very few of us understand the other two.

Made Holy

First of all, the anointing means it is sanctified or made holy. We have just made mention of that. Now, we tend to think of holiness as something terribly drab, sort of colourless, dull, heavy; whereas holiness is not really like that at all. Holiness is connected with soundness and health. It is quite the opposite of what we often think. We often think of holiness as something abnormal, almost diseased. You know the kind of thing. We think of something that is holy as being terribly dark and heavy, and awfully weird, somehow not normal, not a normal human being. But God's idea of holiness is something which is absolutely, in a right way from His point of view, normal, healthy, and sound. What He means is this: it is set apart.

Now, the word "saint" comes from this. I do not know how you would say it, we just cannot say it, but if we could, it would be something like "holite," someone who is holy, a "holyite." But we do get the word "sanctify," which is the same word, to be made holy, and "saint" comes from *sanctify*. We know that we do not become saints at the end of a long struggle. We are made saints by a spiritual birth and by the indwelling of the Lord Jesus. We are called saints. We are sanctified. It is not just a few of the believers who are sanctified. Every born-again believer is sanctified. We ought to enter into the meaning of it, and the experience of it, but every single believer is in fact sanctified. Now, that I think is very important.

Under Direct Authority

The second thing about anointing is that it means that whatever the holy anointing oil touches, that thing or person is under direct authority, the direct authority of God. Now, if the king was anointed, it meant under the old covenant that king was not to be a king like the kings of the other nations, but he was to be the vice regent of God. He was to be the very means by which God ruled, not only that nation, but expressed His government and authority to the nations round about the people of God. If it was a priest, he was not just to be a religious figure, he was to be someone who represented God to the people and the people to God. He was under divine authority.

The prophet, oh, how many times it comes in the Word, the prophet was not to speak his own words. Indeed, I have often thought we would have solved many of our problems today, if the old scriptural injunction was carried out that anyone who prophesied something that did not come to pass should be stoned to death. Now, why was God so very severe on this matter? Because He would not warrant and would not have anything said in His name, which was not really from Him. In other words, the prophet was not just a babbler. He was not just a preacher. He was not someone with the gift of the gab, someone with an amazing capacity for eloquence and oratory. A prophet was someone sent by God with a burden, which was inspired and conceived by the Holy Spirit, and he spoke in the name of the living God. He was under divine authority and divine government.

Now, that explains that extraordinary little instance in the Old Testament where you have an old man who was supposed to be a prophet, and a young man who was a prophet. Do you remember? The old man said to him, "I also have the word of the Lord. Did God say to you that you should pass through this territory and not speak to anybody? I also have the word of the

Lord, listen to me, "You shall stay with me this night."(See 1 Kings 13:9–24) The young prophet stayed with him, and he died. Do you remember the story? Why was God so severe? Because he had no business to do anything that was outside of divine authority and direction. In other words, this being anointed has with it a very real responsibility. It is a most wonderful thing to be under divine authority and direction, under divine government, but it is also a responsibility.

Divine Grace and Divine Power

The third thing about anointing, I think everybody here probably knows. It is that it gives a provision of divine grace and divine power. Now, I think everybody knows that anointing goes with power and it goes with a special grace. If God anoints you for a particular job, He gives you both the grace and the power to do it. Well, I find that rather marvellous.

We come back to this little text now, "It is like the precious oil upon the head, that ran down the beard, even Aaron's beard that came down to the skirt of his garments." Upon the head, it was Aaron's head, the high priest. If you look at Exodus 29:7, we read, "Then shalt thou take the anointing oil and pour it upon his head and anoint him." Now, this was said of Aaron. If you look at Leviticus 8:12, we read again, "And he poured of the anointing oil upon Aaron's head and anointed him to sanctify him."

It is a very interesting thing. Listen to this carefully. The high priest had the anointing oil poured on his head, but the priests, the sons of Aaron, had only the oil sprinkled on them. This is very interesting because Psalm 133 makes a big point about this. In the Hebrew it says, "It is like the precious oil upon *the* head," emphasizing the head, "that ran down upon the beard, even Aaron's beard that came down upon the skirt of his garments". In other words, this is not just anybody. This is a particular head, and a particular beard. It was a particular office, a particular person that was being anointed. So, we take note of that; that is the next thing.

The Skirt of His Garments

Then will you notice this "came down upon the skirt of his garments." Some of you have got the Revised Standard Version, and you will see that it says, "came down upon the collar of his robe," or "of his garments." The New American Standard Bible says, came down or "descended upon the edges of his garments." Now we have a difficulty here because, in actual fact, the word in Hebrew is "mouth." It says the holy oil or the precious oil upon the head ran down the beard, even Aaron's beard, and came upon the *mouth* of his garment. Remember the gentleman then wore, like the good Scots, a kilt sort of thing. They did not wear trousers, so you had holes like a mouth.

This word is translated in different ways. It is, for instance, used again and again in the Old Testament for the edge of the sword, the mouth of the sword, really, if we were to translate it literally. Sometimes it is a word that is used for edge. Sometimes it is the word used for border. In fact, it is even used from end to end of a city, from mouth to mouth, from opening to opening. For men to enter the land, from mouth to mouth, from end to end, as it were, where you come in, and where go out. So, what does it mean? Why does the Authorized Version say the skirt of his garment? Why does my version say the skirt of his garments? It is partly because we really have a problem.

If you turn to Exodus 28:32, this is speaking about this very garment that the high priest is to wear, "And it shall have a hole for the head in the midst thereof: it shall have a binding of woven work round about the hole of it, as it were the hole of a coat of mail, that it be not rent." In Hebrew, this word "hole" is "mouth." Well, some people's mouths are holes. It is quite logical Hebrew in this way. That hole of his garment for his head to go through. Then it goes on using another word, "and upon the skirts of it, thou shalt make pomegranates of blue, and of purple and of scarlet, round about the skirts thereof." We have this twice, not only here, but also in Exodus 39. Why, therefore, does the Authorized Version translate it "skirt" and why do the English Revised and the Old Standard Version that I use, which are very accurate translations, why do they keep to the old version of "skirt"? It is partly because of the Septuagint.

The Septuagint is the oldest translation of the Hebrew Old Testament known to us. It comes from about the second century, roughly, before Christ. Sometimes when they use the Greek word, they were able to use a word more specific than a Hebrew word. When it comes to this Psalm in the Greek, which the early church used, it uses a Greek word meaning the woollen border of a garment, and really the fringe of a garment, the lower fringe of a garment, meaning the skirt. So, whether that befogs you, confuses you, I have no idea. But if we were to read now the Hebrew as it is, it would apparently be "collar." It is like the precious oil upon the head that ran down the beard, even Aaron's beard that came down upon his collar. But then when we look at it a little more closely, it would seem as if it took in the whole. Now whatever is meant, one matter becomes very clear. The oil upon the head runs down to the body. That is the point. Whether it goes down to the hem, or whether it comes to the collar, it comes to the body.

The Oil Runs Down to the Body

Then another very interesting thing you must remember is that upon the high priest's shoulders, upon that very garment, were those twelve precious onyx stones. On each of them was engraved the name of one of the twelve tribes. On his heart, over his whole breast, were twelve precious stones, each one engraved with one of the names of the tribes of the children of Israel. In other words, the oil upon the head that comes down the beard, comes onto the body and includes every member of the covenant people. When the high priest is anointed, it is as if God is saying, "I have every single one of my covenant people in mind. They are before Me. I am sanctifying the whole lot in this one man. I cannot let them all come into the holy place, only the high priest. But when the high priest comes in, they all come in in him." Do you understand? Well, I think that transforms the whole feeling about it.

Then, what about "upon the beard, even Aaron's beard"? I have the greatest sympathy with people who read their scriptures with an open mind and a questioning mind. Surely, you must be terribly dumb, and very, sort of lustreless if you can read a Psalm like this, and not wonder what on earth has happened to it. I mean, what on earth has brethren dwelling together in unity to do with Aaron's beard? Some people do not like beards anyway. What is Aaron's beard doing mixed up with people dwelling together in unity? Then later there is the dew of Hermon. Of course, those of you who are older in the Lord, you all sort of look very contentedly, saying, "Of course, we understand; it is marvellous." But I mean, if you are just young in the Lord, you must think: this is the most extraordinary hodgepodge of a Psalm I have ever read. What has some person's beard got to do with brethren dwelling together in unity, especially someone who lived a thousand years before?

Well, this is so wonderful when you realise it. The anointing oil was not to touch the flesh. So, the Holy Spirit inspires the Psalmist to say it is like the precious oil upon the head that ran down the beard, it never touched his flesh, but via the beard, it comes to the body without touching the flesh. Do you understand? It comes right down to the body. In other words, it is emphasized that the oil upon the head is for the body. This is of tremendous importance if you and I are going to understand why it is like brethren dwelling together in unity, why this is a key to brethren dwelling together in unity, how it becomes an illustration of brethren dwelling together in unity. We have to understand that the oil on the head has a lot to do with the members of the body. Then when we begin to understand that, suddenly, we have a key to brethren dwelling together in unity. The whole Psalm becomes dynamic. It becomes an avenue into fresh light, new truth.

The Indwelling and Empowering of the Holy Spirit

Let us take, therefore, a look at this whole matter. We have looked at the text; let us just have a little look at the whole thing.

First, I want just to underline the vital significance of the person and work of the Holy Spirit. The anointing oil is a symbol of the person and work of the Holy Spirit. There can be no genuine, dwelling together of brethren in unity, apart from the Holy Spirit. It is impossible. We need not only His indwelling, making Christ a reality to us and in us, but we also need his empowering for keeping the unity, His empowering for building up the body of the Lord Jesus. You can know doctrine on this matter, and you can recite it, you could even teach it and yet live in total division with your brothers and sisters. Only the Holy Spirit can keep us alive to the blind spots in ourselves, to those areas of darkness that sometimes are within ourselves and within our own ministry. Only He can do that.

I have travelled quite a bit in the work of God and seen and heard many things. One of the things that appals me more than anything else are good brethren, who will pour out all kinds of things to you, but who are not aware of their own factious spirit. Always it goes back to this question of the person and work of the Holy Spirit.

How can the house of God be built up? How can the body of Christ function and grow to the full-grown man? How can we be perfected into oneness apart from the person and work of the Holy Spirit? When you begin to really look at some of these scriptures, if I may just take you to them, they are very well known to you. But if I could just put my finger on a few phrases, and bring it home to you in that way.

For instance, here are well known verses in Ephesians 2:21, "… in whom the whole building fitly framed together, groweth into a holy temple in the Lord." Now dear ones, how can it be fitly framed together, growing into a holy temple in the Lord apart from the person and work of the Holy Spirit? It is impossible. You can have a doctrine and not a thing happens. So we have to say, "Well, it has been done somehow up there, because really, we have no experience down here of this fitly framing together and growing into our holy temple in the Lord. Then look at this next verse, "... in whom ye also are builded together for a habitation of God in the Spirit." Builded together for a habitation of God in the Spirit.

Look at Ephesians 4:3, "... giving diligence to keep the unity of the Spirit in the bond of peace." Look at verse 12, "... for the perfecting of the saints, unto the work of ministering, unto the building up of the body of Christ, till we all attain unto the unity of the faith, and with the knowledge of the Son of God, unto a full-grown man unto the measure of the stature of the fullness of Christ." Now how is that possible? It is impossible, apart from the person and work of the Holy Spirit. Look at verse 15 and 16: "... but speaking truth in love, may grow up in all things into him, who is the head, even Christ; from whom all the body fitly framed and knit together through that which every joint supplieth, according to the working in due measure of each several part, maketh the increase of the body unto the building up of itself in love." Now, you know as well as I do that you ought to be properly working, but apart from the person and work of the Holy Spirit, it is a doctrine. You are far too self-conscious, far too bound, far too tied up, far too inhibited. It is impossible. You can blame the preacher, you can blame the meeting, you can blame the saints, you can blame the teaching, but in actual fact, in the end, it comes down to ourselves, doesn't it? We know that somewhere in us there is a bondage, there is an inhibition. We know the truth. We know what should happen, but how to break out of just a mental appreciation of truth into a living experience of it? Only the Holy Spirit can break that sound barrier. I emphasize this because to me, it is so important.

When we turn to John 17:21, and hear those wonderful words of our Lord Jesus, we call it the High Priestly prayer. We read, "... that they may all be one; even as thou, Father, art in me, and I in thee, that they also may be in us: that the world may believe that thou didst send me." What a wonderful thing it is when the saints are really growing in that unity, dwelling in it! Then the world knows that God sent the Son. Preaching has a new quality; we do not have to be all the time trying to persuade them. There is something in the very atmosphere by which the Holy Spirit witnesses to an unsaved heart: the Father sent the Son to be the Saviour of the world.

Look here again; read what He says in verses 22 and 23a "... the glory which thou hast given me I have given unto them; that they may be one, even as we are one; I in them, and thou in me, that they may be perfected into one." First, we have the foundational, a fundamental unity, and then we have the being perfected into one. But you know, it is one thing to say, "Oh, we are all one; we are all one." It is another thing to be perfected into one, all the dead flies out of the ointment, all the things that somehow destroy the harmony and so on. Oh, that is another thing. That is where the nitty gritty comes and that is where we get all upset. I think this is important.

It is no coincidence that Zechariah chapter four, speaking about the house being completed, speaking about the lampstand of pure gold, says in verse six, "not by might, nor by power, but by my spirit, saith the LORD of hosts." You cannot just build it because you have seen it in the Bible. That is the first thing. It is not only to see it in the Bible as a teaching, but to have it revealed to you by the Spirit, so it comes by illumination, by enlightenment, then it gets into you. But the third thing is how to realise what you see, how to be practically involved in what you see, how to see that top stone brought forth, finally, with shouts of grace, grace unto it. Only by the Spirit! There is no other way. "Not by might, nor by power, but by My Spirit."

The simple fact, learned from bitter experience, is that without the Holy Spirit, there is an inability to overcome problems. This comes from my own bitter experience. There is an inability. You may know that Christ is Lord, and in the end you become almost sick, may He forgive me, of the truth because somehow it does not work. You hear people talking, talking, talking, but when it comes to you, it does not work. It never will work until the Holy Spirit gets you through the sound barrier.

I used to say years ago, when we were in Egypt, there are only two or three ways that a believer can go on. They either go back altogether into the world, or they become a hypocrite, an unwilling, unwitting hypocrite because they begin to profess things that just do not work in their own lives. Or, by the grace of God, the Holy Spirit brings them through into an experience of both the cross and His work and they come into the reality, a progressive reality. Now, this is true, even of a company like this. We can coast along with people. We can coast along because of the teaching, the singing, and the momentum of the life of the company. But actually, in actual fact, we may not have it inside ourselves. In the end, it all comes down to that. We have got to face it. It has got to be inside me. It has got to be inside you.

From bitter experience, one has learned that there is an inability to overcome problems, whether personal, family, local, national, or international. You just cannot do it without the Holy Spirit. More than that, there is an inability to know the mind of God in practical terms. Oh my, how I see this when I go around in the work of God. You see, you find people who know the Lord, they love the Lord, and they are serving the Lord. But to know the mind of the Lord, in practical terms, this is extremely difficult. People look at you as if you are crazy. They say "but how? I mean, it is so mystical to get on your knees. We have got to use common sense, haven't we?"

We all can see what common sense has done to the work of God. It has well nigh destroyed it because of course, common sense is one of the rarest of all commodities. I mean, you just do not find it. Common sense, frankly, is this: If you have got real common sense, it would tell you that if you have a Head, who is enthroned at the right hand of God, and the Holy Spirit given to join you to the Head, who knows all things in whom are hid all the treasures of wisdom and knowledge, and in whom the very mind of God is personified, well, common sense says, get on your knees and ask Him for a revelation. Doesn't it? I mean, common sense says, "Do not do anything. Wait and wait and wait until finally God reveals His mind."

But you see, without the Holy Spirit, people can talk and talk, but they are 'at sea.' Sometimes they will not admit it, but really in their heart of hearts, they would say, if they were honest, "I cannot read the mind of God. I just cannot read it. I do not know how to tell the will of God. I do not know how the Lord is leading." There is an inability to know the will of God and the mind of God. Now you understand why this is all connected with brethren dwelling together in unity. We have an enemy! You do not think he is just going to let brothers have a lovely picnic together and live together, brothers and sisters just moving on? Of course not! He is going to come from within, he is going to come from without until he has destroyed the whole thing. Unless we are alive all the way through to what the Lord would do, and sometimes it is a very simple thing. God would say, "Do this. Do that. Watch this. Watch that." Instantly we know.

I know you have been seeking the Lord about things here in this company. I cannot help feeling that part of it is just on this very thing: carelessness, just simple carelessness. Such a small thing. On the main things, everything is right, but on small things carelessness—carelessness over one another, carelessness over the things of God, carelessness over the things God has given to us and entrusted to us. So that God is saying, "Alright, alright, if you will be careless, then I will be careless." This will wake you up to a very simple fact that we have got to know the Holy Spirit. We can never, in one sense, let our guard down. All the time, we have to watch. Why did the Lord say, "Watch and pray?" It is just this matter. There is an inability to know the mind of God in practical terms, an inability to do the will of God positively, an inability to play our part in the building up of the church. You see, you know that the church has got to be built up; you know the Lord Jesus said, "I will build My church and the gates of hell shall not prevail against it," but there is an inability in oneself to be part of this building up.

Now, we may know all the doctrine, but that does not mean that we can lay down our life. When it comes to it, if brethren are going to dwell together in unity, they have got to lay down their lives. One by one, they will all fall out of the unity because they have got their own life, and it is the "I." That is why this matter of the holy anointing oil comes in. Either you say "I," and everyone else has got to do what "I" say, or there comes a point where you and I have to die in order that the body of Christ be built up. That is the basis. We cannot do that of ourselves. We cannot even take part in prayer, or exercise a gift, or any of these other things apart from the Holy Spirit. Try. The Holy Spirit not only brings us initially into this unity, this oneness of Christ, it is the Holy Spirit who produces our togetherness, our sense of belonging, our sense of the harmony, the flowing together, the service, the ability to really build one another up.

All in Christ

Now I would like to go on to a third thing. I would like just to say something about the anointing upon the head for the whole body. Every single member of the body is included in this anointing upon the head. "It is like the precious oil upon the head, that ran down the beard, even Aaron's beard that came down to the edge of his garments."

Acts 2:32–33 are very well known verses, I think, to most of us: "This Jesus did God raise up, whereof we all are witnesses. Being therefore by the right hand of God exalted, and having received of the Father the promise of the Holy Spirit, he hath poured forth this, which ye see and hear."

Isn't this a marvellous word? It is borne out by the words of our Lord in the gospel of Luke 24:49: "Behold, I send forth the promise of my Father upon you." Behold *I* send forth the promise of My Father upon you. It is almost as if the Lord had in mind Psalm 133: "It is like the precious oil upon the head, that ran down the beard, even Aaron's beard that came down to the edge of his garments." If you are born of God, you are in Christ. If you are in Christ, you are in the Anointed One, whether we use the Hebrew word "Messiah," or the Greek word, "Christ," both mean the same thing, the Anointed One.

Now, I find this the most helpful way to see this: if I am in the Anointed One, surely, the anointing is there for me. If God by His grace has placed me in the Lord Jesus, and He is the Anointed One of God, the Christ of God, then somewhere, there is an anointing for me. His anointing comes down to me. This is precisely what the Scripture says, "He hath obtained the promise of the Father and poured forth this which ye see and hear." It is just as if He, the Anointed One, ascended into heaven, sat down at the right hand of God, the Father, and took the promise of the Holy Spirit and said, "Here, this is for every member of my body." The precious oil upon the head, running down to the edge of the garment.

Now, if you look at the Scripture again, it seems so. Look at II Corinthians 1:21–22: "Now he that establisheth us with you in Christ, and anointed us, is God; who also sealed us, and gave us the earnest of the Spirit." Established, anointed, sealed, given the earnest of the Spirit. All in Christ. *Established, anointed, sealed, given the earnest of the Spirit. All in Christ.* I find that really rather marvellous.

Compare it with 1 John 2:20: "And ye have an anointing from the Holy One, that ye might know all things." Verse 27: "And as for you, the anointing which ye received of him abideth in you," There you have got the same thought again: the head, the body; the head, the members; the precious oil upon the head, running down to the edge of the garment; Christ, the head, the baptiser into the Holy Spirit.

I think so many people have been afraid of that glorious word baptiser or baptism. I know I have been in past years because one felt there was so much hogwash around the thing, so much that was wrong, so much that was somehow complex. However, the fact remains that the Lord Jesus is called the one who baptises into the Holy Spirit. Now, whatever we may feel about the timing of this baptism into the Spirit, the fact remains it is no small thing. Of course, if you believe in sprinkling, then okay. If you believe that baptism is a sprinkling, then I quite understand that you may just have a little bit of experience of the Holy Spirit and that is it. But if you have seen that baptism is an immersion, then this is no small experience. Jesus is the immerser into the Holy Spirit. He is the one who takes a person and immerses them into the person of the Holy Spirit. Now, that is no small thing! Is the Holy Spirit some impersonal agent? No, He is God, the Spirit. The Lord Jesus takes a believer and immerses him into God, the Holy Spirit. That is no experience to be sniffed at. That is nothing to be derided or devalued or put away somehow. No!

John the Baptist, when describing his own ministry, came to the heart of it by saying, "I baptise with water unto repentance, but He that comes after me baptises with the Holy Spirit [or into the Holy Spirit] and into fire." Matthew 3:11. In other words, the heart of the matter of John's baptism was repentance and the heart of the matter of the ministry of the Lord Jesus is to bring us into the Holy Spirit. What does it mean? It means that He brings us into Himself in reality because there is no other way to know the Lord Jesus in reality, and the things of the Lord Jesus in reality, apart from the person of the Holy Spirit.

I say, oh, if we could only enter into the full meaning of that! I would be the happiest person in the world if everyone here was in the real, full meaning of this being baptised into the Holy Spirit and into fire. I do not mean swinging on lamps and rolling on the floor and making all that noise that some go in for. I mean, maybe sometimes it has to happen, I do not know. But what I do know is this, that once the Holy Spirit really comes upon you, once the Lord Jesus takes a believer and the Holy Spirit, and immerses the little believer into the Holy Spirit, something happens to that person's life, and no one can tell me that is not so. For the first time, you have fragrance. For the first time you sense, not the person, but the Lord Jesus. For the first time you touch the life of God. For the first time you see they have an ability, in all their problems and circumstances, to glorify the Lord. For the first time, they become the means by which others find the Lord. Something has happened. If brethren are going to dwell together in unity and the purpose of God for them is to be fulfilled, no wonder it is like the precious oil upon the head that ran down the beard. There is no doubt about it.

This anointing is ours in Christ, and it is ours through Christ. Now I make a distinction there. It is ours *in* Christ, and it is ours *through* Christ. If we are in the Anointed One, and that is our position, it is ours. There must be a portion of His anointing which is ours. But it is also ours through Christ, not my own effort. Oh, many a dear saint who has gone on with the Lord has made such a hash of things just on this point. They felt that somehow or other if they fast for days on end and turn over new leaves and become very zealous and do this and do that God will sort of say, "Oh, my word, So-and-So is trying so hard; I will have to do something." But in actual fact, what we have done is we have substituted grace for works and unwittingly, have barred the doors of heaven to ourselves. It is not that we should not fast, not that we should not seek, not that we should not pray, not that we should not get things cleared up as far as God enables us, but those things do not bring us into a real experience of the anointing. We had the anointing through grace, simply because He died for us and because His finished work is sufficient for every single claim. Praise God! Nevertheless, we need to enter in, by faith, to what is ours in Him. It is perfectly true, that on the basis of Christ's finished work, and our position in Him, He anoints us. Did you ever realise that? It is not a preacher that anoints you, or a teaching that anoints you, and nor do you yourselves get an anointing. In actual fact, He always anoints. Anything else is counterfeit. It is emotional, transient, passing away. When the Lord anoints, it is something done.

Entering the Anointing By Faith

Having said that, I have to contradict it by saying this: we need to enter in by faith to what is ours in Him and if we do not, we do not experience the anointing. Now, we come to the heart of the problem for many I know. When do we experience the anointing which is ours in Christ? Oh, my! People get so heated up on this problem, and so divided. When do we experience the anointing which is ours in Christ? I have a fool proof answer to this: whenever by faith we enter in. It is as simple as that. If you want to enter in at conversion, you can, if you understand it. I have known some, very few, but I have known some who at their conversion have known an anointing, and the two things have gone together. My word, what a strong birth that has been. How glorious it has been to watch them! But generally speaking, it follows conversion with the vast majority of us. I could, of course, if we had time, read to you from the life stories of all the great ones in the history of the church. You will find the same thing in all of them. Some will say, "Well, it is because people were not taught properly." Maybe, but the answer is this: when do we experience this anointing? Whenever by faith, we enter in to what is ours in the Lord!

When I am asked, "Is this a distinct experience?" I always answer by asking a question: "Are you in the good and the reality of this anointing?" You see, I think, those who have got a more theological background, we get so tied up on these things. Our first thing is, "Is this a distinct experience? Does it come after conversion?" Then we are just waiting for somebody to say, "yes," and then we say, "I cannot understand that. I just cannot understand it. How?" That is to miss the whole point!

Oh, the angels must weep over us at times. The real question is this: "Okay, okay. Why argue about theology? Are you in the good of the anointing?" If you have to say to me, "No, I'm not," then I say, "Well, then you have got to enter in, haven't you?" It is no good saying, "Oh, well, yes, but I think it was mine." Then I say, "Well, you just said you are not in the good of it. You are living a defeated life, an unhappy life. You are inhibited. You can't take part in prayer. You can't witness to other people, you can't lead someone else to the Lord. You have never really been involved in the building up of the church. You haven't got the power over habits in your life. You can't settle issues in your life. You can't lay down your life for the brethren. But you say that you are anointed!"

Heaven must sit down and weep. Okay, you are anointed. Officially. If you want to look at it like that, okay, you are anointed officially. Does heaven go on official things? Do you think God will say to you, "Now, I want you to go to the Philippines," or "I will send you here? I don't know where, but somewhere." Then the Lord says to you, "You have got an official anointing, you know." So, you say, "That ought to be sufficient." Then you go out to face demons and spirits, and Satan and the powers of darkness and somehow or other you have only got an official anointing. Don't you think hell will laugh at you? Don't you think it will be a joke amongst the evil spirits? "Ha! So-and-So has got an official anointing!" Of course, it is true, but you are not in the good of it.

So then, the fact of the matter is this: are you in the good of it? If someone comes to me and says, "Well, you know, I was converted, and at the moment I was converted, I knew a power to pray, and I have become an intercessor." I say, "Thank God, the Lord has anointed you." But when a person comes to me and says, "I can't do this, I can't do that, and I can't do the other, and the Lord has called me to this, and I just can't do it. I am just going around the bend over the whole thing," I know they have no anointing—

practically. It is theirs in Christ. Their position is in Christ. What are we to do with them? Are we to play theology with them? Are we to leave them in the barrenness? Are we to leave them in a land of aridity, powerless before the powers of darkness? Or are we to say to them, "Dear one, be practical. Something has gone wrong. You need to seek the Lord that you may come into what is yours in Him."

One thing is abundantly clear, and I imagine that nearly everybody, if not every single person in this room will agree with me on this. We all know an anointed preacher, we all know an anointed leader, and we all know an anointed member of the body. Now that person may not know themselves, but we all know, don't we? My goodness, we can hear someone preaching and we think: "Marvellous words! Tremendous truth," but it doesn't do anything. It just does not do anything. There is no anointing. It is the same with leadership. It is the same with a member in the body of Christ. We can be a dear member of the body of Christ, a real member of the body of Christ, and yet somehow we are not giving. We don't bring life in. We don't exercise what is ours. We don't share the Lord with us in a way that others are built up.

Oh, but we know people who have got an anointing. We do not even perhaps have to call it technically an anointing. We just know in our spirit. We say, "You know, So-and-So has got it. Listen to them pray. They are on the ball. There is an authority in their prayer. Listen to the way they exercise faith. That does not come naturally. That does not come through studying. That is an anointing."

It is so in everything. You know, even the world, may it shame us, even the world can tell an anointed preacher. They will say,

"You know So-and-So, that person has got something." What they mean is that "something" is unction from above.

Certainly, our Lord Jesus was born of the Spirit, but He was 30 years of age when He was anointed of the Holy Spirit. He said in the synagogue at Nazareth, "This day is this Scripture fulfilled before your eyes, and in your ears. The Spirit of the Lord God is upon me, because he has anointed me to preach good tidings to the meek." Luke 4:18a. It says in Acts 10:37–38, "... you know ... that after the baptism which John preached, Jesus of Nazareth, anointed with the Holy Spirit, went around doing good, healing the sick," and so on.

It is also as clear that the prophet, priest, and king were all anointed long after being in a covenant relationship with God. They could not be sort of made covenant members of the nation, and then immediately anointed. They were born and circumcised, they already were part of the covenant people, and then they were anointed. Now this is not to say that under the new covenant, we have to wait a great long time between when we are born of God, and when we are anointed by God. However, what I am saying is this: there is nothing theological that stands against it. It is ours in the Lord.

I think also it is true and very instructive to note Exodus 29:20–21, speaking about the anointing of the priests. You will notice that first the blood is put on them, and then the oil. You have this same thing to do with leprosy and it is very strange. It is the right ear, the right thumb and the big toe, the right big toe. Isn't that interesting? First blood—blood on the ear (what you hear), on the thumb (what you do), and on the toe (where you go). Then the oil was put on the ear, on the thumb, and on the toe. Many a believer knows all about the blood but does not know anything about the Spirit. The two must go together. It was so with the priests. It is so even with the sinner, the picture of the sinner saved by the grace of God.

It is also very clear, may I say, that the Lord Jesus went to great pains to make a distinction between the indwelling of the Spirit and the empowering of the Spirit. When you read in John 20:21–22, you remember He breathed upon them and said, "Receive ye the Holy Spirit." Now He knew very well the Holy Spirit was not actually given. So, what happened? Well, some people say, "Well, they actually received the Holy Spirit." Well, if they did, it was strange, because Thomas was not there. When Thomas came, He never breathed on him and said, "Now, Thomas, you have been left out of this, you must receive the Holy Spirit." No. It is quite clear to me that it was a symbolic act, at least as I see it. But what was our Lord doing? He knew that on the day of Pentecost the Holy Spirit, at the beginning of the dispensation, came within and upon at the same time. All He wanted to do was to make clear in those apostle's minds, that there is a distinction, not necessarily in time, but a distinction that must be made between the indwelling and the empowering of the Holy Spirit. These are two aspects of the Holy Spirit's work. He is inside and upon.

It is interesting that having said that, "Receive ye the Holy Spirit," Acts 1:3–5 says after that, "to whom He also showed Himself alive after his passion by many proofs, appearing unto them by the space of forty days, and speaking the things concerning the kingdom of God: and, being assembled together with them, He charged them not to depart from Jerusalem, but to wait for the promise of the Father, which, said He, ye heard from me: for John indeed baptised with water; but ye shall be baptised in the Holy Spirit not many days hence." In other words, He breathed the Holy Spirit into them, that was at the indwelling, at least the distinction He was making. Then He said, "You shall be baptised into the Holy Spirit." This is to be all upon you, immersed in Him.

Well, now, I say all this because I think it is very, very important for us to understand this connection between this precious oil and brethren dwelling together in unity. The fact is simply this: the Word of God commands us to be filled with the Holy Spirit. Be filled with the Holy Spirit, now it says actually, "Be being filled." If it is not true of me, I ought to start to wake up and seek Him.

The Consequences of Anointing

Now, let me just ask, in closing, what are the consequences of this anointing? There are just four things. I will only mention them because we have said a lot about them at other times.

Power

The first consequence is power. Acts 1:8, "Ye shall receive power, when the Holy Spirit has come upon you." Oh, that is a marvellous thing to receive the power to do the will of God. The power to be what God wants you to be. The power to go where God wants you to go. The power to speak what God gives you to speak. Power. Power to be a living sacrifice, underlying the whole. I would never, ever devalue that.

Fullness

Here is the second thing, fullness. Ephesians 5:18 and this other verse, Matthew 3:11, "... baptised into the Holy Spirit," "... be filled with the Spirit." It is interesting that it says when you are filled with the Spirit, you will sing, making melody in your heart. Something happens. Fullness. Lost in His fullness. It says, "All the fullness of the Godhead dwells in him bodily and ye are made full in him." Colossians 2:9. Oh, to be in that reality! Fullness of resources, fullness of energy, fullness of wisdom, fullness of grace. It is all there. That is a consequence of anointing, divine grace and divine power provided.

Clothing

The third thing is clothing. Remember Luke 24:49? "Ye shall be clothed with power from on high." Better than endued with power from on high, clothed with power from on high. What does this mean? Of course, you are clothed when you are saved, when you are justified, that is the garment of your salvation. This clothing means to be rightly clothed for the job. When you are wrongly clothed for a job, you are very self-conscious because all the time you are thinking about your clothing. You ladies would not think of putting your most expensive dress on and cooking, especially if you are frying something. Can you imagine? You would be sort of conscious of yourself all the time. You cannot be thinking of the meal you are doing because you are conscience of your clothing. You boys, especially if you have got a little bit of self-respect, would not think of getting under a car in your best suit. You would think all the time of your best suit.

Do you understand? When you are rightly clothed, you are not self-conscious. You just have no self-consciousness at all.

I have told you the story before, most of you know it, of the marvellous occasion, quite a few years ago now. On a Sunday evening, I sped across the bridge here for the 6:30 gospel service. I got to the brothers—no one said they noticed anything odd about me—we got down in prayer. We were praying, and when I got up I just looked down. We had about seven minutes to go before the service and I said, "Ohhh!" Everyone looked, and I said, "I've got my red slippers on!" I remember they said, "Well, no one will ever notice," but I said, "Oh, yes they will!" I could not go. I could only think of myself on that platform and any brother or sister who was devotedly praying, bowing their head. I would immediately think about my feet, and them saying, "Wearing red shoes, whatever next?"

Some kind brother had a bike, sped across the bridge to my home, upstairs into my room, took my shoes, fled back across the bridge, and my feet went into the shoes, I think I was just a minute or two late. In we went and I preached. You know, I never thought about my feet. Now, if I had had those red shoes, I would have spent the whole time thinking about my feet, especially if anyone happened to sort of look. They might have seen a fly buzzing around, but I would have been sure it was my feet. I would have lost my thread, forgotten the message because I was conscious only of myself. But I never thought of myself. All I thought about was the message that God had given me. When you are rightly clothed, you do not think about yourself; you can think about the job you have got to do. That is the beauty of the anointing. It means that you are freed from introspection and self-consciousness, to do the job God has given you to do.

Equipment

The fourth thing about the consequences of the anointing is equipment. 1 Corinthians 12:4: "There are diversities of gifts, but one spirit ... to each one is given the manifestation of the Spirit to profit withal." (verse 7) "Earnestly desire the better gifts," it says in verse 31.

Gifts are never to be seen in contradistinction to Christ, (you can either have Christ or the gifts). I have heard people sometimes say to me, very spiritually, "Oh, I do not want gifts; I want Christ." Well, if they mean sort of exhibitionism, I quite understand. However, that is not how I see gifts; I see gifts as a gift of Christ. It is something of Christ expressed in you. When it is faith, it is Christ expressing faith in you. When it is a word of wisdom or knowledge, it is Christ expressing one of those treasures of wisdom and knowledge that has spilled over into you and coming out for us. What a tremendous thing it is in prayer, when a word of wisdom comes about a situation we are facing or a word of knowledge about the facts. It is tremendous. I think it is.

I am personally very glad for that dear old lady in America who was tipped out of bed by the Lord at 2 AM in the morning and given a word of knowledge about me. I am very thankful for it; it did not happen to anybody else. I am just thankful that the Lord got her out of bed, gave her a word of knowledge, and got her working. There was an example of an anointing for you. Praise the Lord for it! It had consequence.

I was in a conference a year or two ago and we were waiting, queuing up for meals. This brother turned around to me and said, "You know," he said, "I want the Lord, not gifts. I want Jesus." I said to him, "Oh brother, that is beautiful." I said, "So do I. I want Jesus. But," I said, "I don't see the gifts quite like that. I see gifts as Him." He looked at me very surprised. I think he said, "Oh dear, don't tell me you're charismatic." Then he muttered a bit and I said to him, "You see brother, if I had appendicitis and was rushed into hospital," I said, "I wouldn't be terribly thrilled if you told me that the surgeon operating on me had gone to such-and-such a medical college to be trained and had all those letters after his name if I saw him coming at me with a tree saw and a chisel. I would say, 'Oh! I'm not the least bit bothered about his title and where he was trained, I want to know what is his equipment!'"

It is so stupid when you really see it. I mean, people say, "We don't want gifts. We don't want gifts. We want the Lord." The point is what they really mean is this: we only want part of the Lord. We want the Lord without His gifts. Which means that we are poorer. It means that when we are facing real problems in the work of God, we have not got the equipment to do the job. No wonder this scripture says, "brethren dwelling together in unity." There are going to be problems. Do you not think that the enemy will try to intrude upon the well-being of the brothers and sisters, that he will not attack them mentally? That he will not attack them physically? I am not saying that every sickness is enemy inspired, and that every single thing has got to be healed. I am not saying that. What I am saying is this, that the enemy is the master of much of it. When the saints know how to deal with it, or other things, not just on the matter of the mental side, or the physical side but so often on other things where the enemy perplexes, frustrates, wears out, ties up, brings in knotty problems that are so complex that no one can unravel them. What are we to do? We are worn out. That is what happens because we have not got the equipment, but the anointing gives us the equipment.

The Anointing is Not to Touch the Flesh

Well, there we are. I hope that has been of some help to you. This anointing is not to touch the flesh. What damage and harm has been done to the work of God, when the flesh has entered into this realm. Gifts used in the flesh. Exhibitionism, just self-interest, ambition, and sometimes people's own will and opinion put into a "Thus says the Lord." What damage is done! The end, when the flesh comes in, is always the same: disintegration, division, and death. When, however, there is a right division between soul and spirit, then brethren dwell together in unity and the purpose of God is realised. May the Lord help us. If you have got needs in your life, seek the Lord. Let Him just open you up in a very real way to Himself. It is yours in Him, if you will only take that step forward.

Let us pray:

Dear Lord, we have been talking about this holy anointing oil upon the head, that ran down to the very hem of the garment. Oh, Lord, we come to Thee, and we tell Thee Lord, whether we have had experience of the anointing or not, we long, Lord, for that anointing. If we have had an anointing, we long for a deeper anointing, Lord and if we have never known the anointing, we long, Lord, that we might know it, not for ourselves, not to be misspent, but, Lord, that we might be those who serve Thee with gladness. In these days in which we are living Lord, days in which the enemy is seeking to wear out the saints, oh Lord, we praise Thee for the work of Thy Holy Spirit. Grant, Lord, we pray, that we may all know the depths and the fullness of this anointing, both individually and together as Thy people. We ask this in the name of our Lord Jesus. Amen.

4.
The Dew of Hermon upon the Mountains of Zion

Psalm 133

*Behold, how good and how
pleasant it is for brethren to
dwell together in unity!
It is like the precious oil upon
the head,
That ran down upon the beard,
Even Aaron's beard;*

*That came down upon the skirt
of his garments;
Like the dew of Hermon,
That cometh down upon the
mountains of Zion:
For there the Lord commanded
the blessing, Even life for
evermore.*

I want to take the last verse in Psalm 133. We have already spent three times on this little Psalm. We spent two times upon the first verse, and one on the second verse. Now we come to this last verse.

You will remember that this little Psalm, one of the shortest in the whole psalter, might well give us a question, as some who do not believe in the authority and inspiration of the word as we have it, as to whether quite a number of verses have fallen out of the Psalm. To a critical mind, it does not make sense. Brethren dwelling together in unity, and Aaron's beard, and oil running down his head upon his beard, to the skirt of his garment—what on earth has it got to do with brothers dwelling together in unity? Then dew coming down from Mount Hermon upon the mountains of Zion. It just seems absolutely extraordinary. One feels as Dr. Moffat used to feel, that perhaps quite a number of verses have fallen out and got misplaced or lost on the way, and that finally, we have but a very poor skeleton of the original Psalm. However, I trust we have already seen in our previous studies, that this is not so. The Holy Spirit, with great care, has composed this little Psalm.

Of course, the first great lesson of this Psalm is the oneness of the brethren. It is brethren, it is not just anybody. It is not human beings. It is brethren—those who have the same parent, the same source, the same origin, the same name. They are brothers. These ones are living together, dwelling together in unity. They are not just experiencing a high point of unity in some conference, or some great sort of get together in the year, but they are *dwelling together* in unity.

Then we spent one whole session on "the precious oil upon the head that ran down upon the beard, even Aaron's beard that came down to the skirt of his garment." Of course, we found that this is the precious anointing oil. It is interesting that it was sprinkled on the rest of the priests, but upon the high priest it was poured, and it was never to touch the flesh. That is why it says it was upon the head and came down the beard onto his garment.

You will remember that on his garment he had the onyx stones upon his shoulders—the six stones and six stones, each with one of the names of the tribes of Israel. All the people of God were on his shoulder; the government upon his shoulder. Then on his heart, over his heart, he had twelve precious stones. Upon each one of those stones was one of the names of the twelve tribes of the covenant people of God. They were borne on his heart. The anointing oil upon the head united the body with the head. Isn't that wonderful?

We spoke at some length about the need of knowing the anointing of the Holy Spirit, whether it is a second experience or not. I will not go over that now. Suffice it to say, there can be really no dwelling together in unity apart from the empowering and anointing of the Holy Spirit. We need the right clothing to be really found together. We need power to stay together. We need power to overcome the problems and difficulties that would divide us, or alienate us, or at least distance us from one another. We need gifts to build one another up. It is not just that we want to all be together in a kind of just disgruntled unity, a kind of, "Well, I have got to put up with you because God has saved you. Therefore, because God has saved you and He saved me, we two have got to stay together, but frankly, we would prefer to be a thousand miles apart."

It seems to me that this kind of thing is not loving thy neighbour as thyself. What we need is something far more positive than that, something that overcomes all that just, "Well, we have *got* to stick together," but really is a positive building of one another up in the Lord, a positive caring for one another in the Lord. I say, that cannot come apart from the anointing of the Holy Spirit. We may be one in the Lord, our position may be in the one Christ and He in us, thank God, but we need the power of the Holy Spirit if we are going to see that unity positively expressed, if we are to be perfected into one. That is the point: "fitly framed and growing together into a holy temple in the Lord." It is one thing just to say we are one. It is another thing to be perfected into one and to grow up into Him who is the head from whom the whole body fitly framed and knit together through that which every joint supplies (Ephesians 4:16).

The Dew of Hermon Upon the Mountains of Zion

Now we come to the dew of Hermon upon the mountains of Zion. *"Like the dew of Hermon, That cometh down upon the mountains of Zion: For there the Lord commanded the blessing, Even life for evermore."* Let us just take a look at the actual text for a moment. Here we are given the second illustration or key to brethren dwelling together in unity. It is introduced by this little word in English, "it is like." In Hebrew, it is just a little one letter of the alphabet, that is all. It introduces both these illustrations in exactly the same way. In English, we have in my version, "it is like the precious oil," and secondly, we have, "like the dew of Hermon." However, in the Hebrew it is exactly the same, "It is like, it is like." We have two illustrations, two keys. Now, we have dealt with one of the keys, which is the precious anointing oil that flows from the head to every member of the body. Now we have the second key, which is all to do with dew.

Dew in Israel

Now dew, being an important feature in the life of ancient Israel, as well as modern Israel, is given quite a place in Scriptures.

We all love to see the dew on a summer morning as we look out upon the lawn, or whatever is there. It is lovely to see the dew. We feel it is a sign of good weather, it is something pleasant and nice. We, of course, have a lot of rain here like last summer. You hardly need any dew with rain like that, but in the East, and particularly in Israel, dew is an essential feature in quite a number of fields. The Bible has very much to say about it.

For instance, in Genesis 27:28: "And God give thee of the dew of heaven, And of the fatness of the earth, And plenty of grain and new wine." It is interesting that he does not say, "God give thee of the **rain** of heaven," but he says, "God give thee of the **dew** of heaven and of the fatness of the earth, and plenty of grain and new wine."

Or again, if you look in Deuteronomy 32:2: "My doctrine shall drop as the rain; My speech," says Moses, "shall distil as the dew." In chapter 33:13 it says, "And of Joseph, he said, Blessed of the Lord be his land, For the precious things of heaven, for the dew, And for the deep that coucheth beneath, And for the precious things of the fruits of the sun, And for the precious things of the growth of the moons," and so on. Isn't it interesting? He says about heaven again, "for the precious things of heaven, for the dew." Then again, in the same chapter, and verse 28: "And Israel dwelleth in safety, The fountain of Jacob alone, In a land of grain and new wine; Yea, his heavens drop down dew." Again, you have got the dew.

If you turn to Judges 6 you may have a little shock. Of course, all of you who ever had a Sunday school upbringing know it I suppose. Judges 6:38: "And it was so; for he," (that is Gideon) "rose up early on the morrow, and pressed the fleece together, and wrung the dew out of the fleece, a bowlful of water."

That is quite a lot of dew. That is some little indication of the heaviness of the dew in an area bordering on what we call the wilderness of Judea. Gideon lived in an area right over toward the east and really, it is quite arid. So, to have so much dew in a fleece that he could wring out a whole bowl of water is some kind of dew.

Then in Isaiah 18:4 you have another reference. (Now you do realize that I am only giving you the tiniest fraction of the references to dew in the Bible.) "For thus hath the Lord said unto me, I will be still, and I will behold in my dwelling-place, like clear heat in sunshine, like a cloud of dew in the heat of harvest."

Now, the cloud of dew is something really quite interesting. I remember in Egypt we used to now and again get this extraordinary cloud-mist early in the morning that just went through and left the trees dripping wet. It was just a mist, drawn up from the dew and then carried along. Quite extraordinary. There you have got it.

Look at Hosea 14:5–6: "I will be as the dew unto Israel;" (Now listen to the consequences of being dew to Israel.) "he shall blossom as the lily, and cast forth his roots as Lebanon. His branches shall spread, and his beauty shall be as the olive-tree, and his smell as Lebanon. They that dwell under his shadow shall return; they shall revive as the grain, and blossom as the vine: the scent thereof shall be as the wine of Lebanon."

All this came out of one single statement, "I will be as the dew unto Israel." Now, dew does not normally do that kind of thing. It may keep things alive, but what a wonderful promise that is that Israel will blossom. This is the Israel that has gone away from the Lord. This is the Israel that has got alienated from the Lord, that has become jaded, faded, barren, arid, tired, and weary. To this Israel, the Lord promises, "I will be as the dew unto Israel; he shall blossom as the lily and cast forth his roots as Lebanon." A tremendous harvest comes out of it, and not only a harvest, but fragrance and shade and everything else for others. Very beautiful.

Then also we have another interesting little verse, a very mysterious verse I might add, in Isaiah 26:19. (We have many different versions; it would be almost interesting to stop here and ask everybody to read what they have got in their different versions.) This is how it is rendered in mine: "Thy dead shall live; my dead bodies shall arise. Awake and sing, ye that dwell in the dust; for thy dew is as the dew of herbs, and the earth shall cast forth the dead."

Now in the Hebrew, "the herbs" can be translated, "the lights," and in the New American Standard Bible I believe it is "the dawn." In other words, "Thy dew is as the dew of the dawn, and the earth shall cast forth the dead." Now, the rabbis said that this was a reference to the great resurrection and I think that must be so. Therefore, you get a very beautiful Talmudic phrase, which probably lies behind a certain amount of the thinking of the Bible on the matter of dew. We have this lovely Talmudic phrase, "the dew of resurrection." The dew of resurrection, meaning that there was a reference that in the end, when God acts, it will be the reviving of things and bringing them back into life again. What a lovely phrase that is: "the dew of resurrection." It seems to me to get right to the heart of this whole matter.

The Geography of Mount Hermon

Now we come to our problems. Come back to Psalm 133:3: "Like the dew of Hermon, that cometh down upon the mountains of Zion." Literally, in Hebrew, "It is like the dew of Hermon, descending on the mountains of Zion." Coming down, descending on the mountains of Zion, what does this mean? You see, all the experts tell us that the dew in Israel, which is such a feature in the dry season and which lasts for six to eight months, is produced by the westerly wind coming in from the sea every day without fail and which distils in a heavy dew during the night.

It might interest you to know that on the coastal plain and right down to Gaza, which is desert in the beginning of Sinai or the Negev, 250 nights out of the 365 nights of the year have a heavy dew. When you get into the hill country, 150 nights to 180 nights have this. Now, 180 nights is six months. That really is some dew, isn't it, when you think about it? However, our problem is that this does not say anything about westerly winds. Hermon is not in the West. I do not know how up you are on your biblical geography or your modern geography for that matter, but Hermon is in the north of the country and the mountains of Zion are in the south of the country, whereas we are told by all the experts that it is the westerly wind driving from the west to the east, which in fact does this.

Now, those of you who know just a little bit about Israel will remember, especially if you have been there in the dry season, that literally, almost like clockwork, between 3:00 and 3:30 every afternoon from May till October, you can be sure that a breeze, a strong breeze, will start. In actual fact, so again the experts tell us, early in the morning there is no breeze at all on the coastal plain.

If you had smoke, it would go straight up. The breeze begins about 9:00 in the morning but does not get to the hill country, that is the mountainous part of Israel where Jerusalem is, till about 3:00 in the afternoon. This westerly mass of air starts to come in and gets there at about 3:00–3:30 in the afternoon, which is very, very welcome for everybody in Jerusalem when you are dying of the heat. It is every single day without fail. Indeed, sometimes in the autumn it can get so cool that you need to put on a woolly after 3:30 if you are up on the Mount of Olives or the French Hill or Mount Scopus or somewhere like that. Now, the point is this: that it then in the evening distils as dew. But this gets us no nearer to what the Bible means because the Bible says, "as the dew of Hermon cometh down upon the mountains of Zion."

Now, very clever ones have pointed out to me, and I remember very well in Egypt, a dear missionary who pointed it out to me many, many years ago, "Oh, there is a simple explanation for this. You will find it in Deuteronomy 4:48: "from Aroer, which is on the edge of the valley of the Arnon, even unto mount Sion (the same is Hermon)." Do you see it? We are told by those who feel that the Bible explains the Bible that here is the key. The dew never did go right the way down to the south. The dew of Hermon remains on Hermon. All it does is come down from the peak to the orchard. This is very, very interesting because, in actual fact, the whole base of Hermon is covered with the most luscious apple orchards, and it really depends upon the dew very largely for the fruit to ripen and to become as sweet as it is famous for.

However, if you look at Deuteronomy 3:9 it says, "Which Hermon the Sidonians call Sirion, and the Amorites call it Senir." Now, here is our whole problem. If you do not understand any

Hebrew, you can accept this explanation. But unfortunately, if you understand a little bit of Hebrew, the whole thing is exploded because the Sion here is spelt with entirely different letters, except the last "n," and it cannot be the Zion. That is why it is Sion. The other is "See-on;" this is Seon. There is a difference, and it is almost certain that it is Sirion because Sirion, which is what the Sidonians called Hermon, in Hebrew is Siron. So, it is probable that either an "r" fell out or ... In other words, this Sion mentioned here is not Zion.

"The Mountains of Zion"

Now, here is my next problem. "The mountains of Zion" is a very interesting phrase. In this Psalm 133:3 it is the only incidence of this use in the whole of the Bible. We read everywhere else, "Mount Zion, Mount Zion, Mount Zion," but here we read of the "mountains of Zion." What does it all mean?

There is another very interesting little explanation. (For those of you who would like to pray about it and follow it through, it certainly has got a lot in it. One day we might think about it a little more.) Even today in Arabic, Hermon is called the Mount of Consecration. In Jewish circles, the Kabbalists, that is the mystic type of Judaism, believe that Hermon represents consecration. Even so godly a man as Bishop William Kaye, points out that Hermon represents consecration. Now, if this is so, and if Zion represents the overcomer—as Brother Nee and Mr. Sparks used to say, "Jerusalem is the people of God, but Zion is where the throne is as government, as the overcomer,"—then you have a very interesting connection between absolute consecration and overcoming. In other words, utterness and getting through.

The only way that you can get through is if you know what it is to be renewed all the time. There is no other way through. Now that may be an explanation.

However, there is one last thing I would like to say in this matter. Mount Hermon is the highest mountain in Israel. It rises to some 9,100 feet. It is snowcapped for much of the year right through to the beginning of June and has great influence upon the rest of Israel. It is the largest single source of the River Jordan which unites the north and the south of the country. You could almost say Mount Hermon and the mountains of Zion, that is the mountains around Jerusalem, are united by the Jordan Valley and the Jordan River. Of course, the mountains of Zion, meaning the mountains round about Jerusalem, and the mountains upon which Jerusalem is built itself are much drier and more arid than Mount Hermon.

Now, those are all the technical sides. It is certainly true that Jerusalem is kept alive and fresh by the regular nightly dew fall throughout the dry season. Any of you who came with me to Jerusalem would know, if we were to visit somebody for half an hour and leave the car outside anywhere in Jerusalem, even the driest part of Jerusalem, right on the edge of the wilderness of Judea, when you come out half an hour later, you will find the car wet with dew. You will have to wipe all the windows before we can even drive off. It is most remarkable.

The dew comes every single night. Indeed, much of the vegetation of Jerusalem, since there was only one source of water other than those wells that have been cut out to catch the rainfall, is watered by the only actual source of refreshing which comes from the dew.

One other little point I might make: from the whole area around Jerusalem, its biggest harvest is grapes. Now, the Muslims do not, of course, drink alcohol, so they are not so keen on producing the vine. But in the old days, in Jewish days, of course, they were very, very keen on wine and the vine. All those areas and all the great wine growing areas were heavily terraced. Now, the grape depends upon the dew to become fully ripe. I think I would have to ask someone about the olive, but I am almost certain that my Arab brothers and sisters have told me that the olive also takes much from the dew to become fleshy and to ripen.

Now, what can we say about this? It seems as if what we are told by experts is not quite borne out by Scripture, in which case on whose side shall we come down? Well, don't look so surprised. I mean, I can only come down on one side and that is Scripture. I have long since discovered that experts mouth their theories and are very interesting, but when they conflict with the Bible, sooner or later the Bible is vindicated, and the experts change their theories entirely. At present, the experts say that although they do not always understand the exact action of dew, yet in Israel it is to do with the westerly winds that come in. All I can say in this matter is that whatever their theories are, whether in fact they will alter their theories, Psalm 133 connects the dew fall of the Jerusalem area with Mount Hermon in the north. Let it be said quite clearly, because some commentators try to get out of it by saying, "I do not think it is necessary to have to feel that Hermon and the mountains of Zion are connected by the dew fall." Well, I have to say that I think it is quite plainly connected. It says, "The dew of Hermon falleth down" or "comes down" or "descends upon the mountains of Zion." So, whether the experts will alter their theories in time to come, we shall see. The fact remains that the Bible connects Mount Hermon in the north and the mountains in the south with the dew fall that comes to both.

The Nature of Dew

Now, what is the nature of the dew? It is "an atmospheric vapour condensed in small drops on cool surfaces from evening to morning." Doesn't that take all the romance out of it? I will repeat it again: an atmospheric vapour condensed in small drops on cool surfaces from evening to morning. This is the Oxford dictionary definition. You may well prefer the old word "dew".

It is quiet, gentle, hidden in operation, continuous, and regular in the dry season in Israel. Above all, it is life giving. It renews, reinvigorates, revives. We have seen this in some of the Old Testament references. For example, the reference I have read to you from Hosea 14:5 about the Lord saying, "I shall be as the dew to Israel, and he shall blossom as the lily," and all the rest that comes out of it.

In New Testament terms, the dew symbolizes the power of Christ's resurrection. As we find it, for instance, in Philippians 3:10, "That I may know him, and the power of his resurrection, and the fellowship of his sufferings, becoming made conformable unto his death." Power of His resurrection. Another wonderful phrase is in Hebrews 7:16, "the power of an endless life." To me, that seems to describe the dew—the power of an endless life, quiet, gentle, hidden in operation, continuous and regular, life giving.

Now, this is the work of the Holy Spirit. We have seen His work in Psalm 133:2, as the precious anointing oil, the oil that comes upon the head of the high priest, that runs down upon his garment. That aspect of His work is dynamic, dramatic, powerful in a manifested way. For instance, do not let anybody tell me that a man can be anointed, and it is not manifested. It is absolute nonsense. He himself may not know it sometimes (although I think even he knows himself that something, by the grace of God, has come upon him and into him), but everybody else knows it. No one is going to tell me that a believer, however stupid, cannot tell the difference between an anointed preacher and unanointed preacher, or between an anointed leader and an unanointed leader, or an anointed member of the body and an unanointed member of the body.

The fact of the matter is that when this anointing comes upon a person, something happens. Even when the anointing came upon Saul and those silly men that were with him, they all prophesied. Their intent and motives were evil and murderous, but they all prophesied. When the anointing came upon Balaam's ass, he prophesied! I mean, there is a manifestation in this matter of precious anointing oil.

Now, some people say, "Well, I have never prophesied." Yes, but you see, there comes a new authority in your prayer. You begin to take hold of things in prayer. You were never able to do that before. In your whole way with the Lord there is a definite, clear-cutness that was never there before. You see, this anointing brings with it something that is quite manifest. It is manifested in a public way. Any man or woman who is anointed by the Spirit of God, it is manifested very soon, in a public way.

Of course, I have said dramatic. I know a lot of damage has been done to the use of gifts by this kind of artificial, dramatic use of them. I did not mean that. What I mean is that the anointing itself is dramatic. A man may be just so dull, so heavy, so wooden, and then suddenly, one day you get him back and he is a different man! It is dramatic.

I can tell you of all kinds of people I have met, for I am convinced about this matter. I have known people you could not have fellowship with. I knew they were believers, but you could not have fellowship with them. You just had to spend the time of day with them, that is all; mutter about this, and that, and the other. It was all very hard going. Then, suddenly, they come and they are full of fellowship. They are hungry. They are alive. They do not have to say to you, "Listen, I went to such and such a place and God has met me." You can see it, you know it, it is dramatic. It is dynamic. Something has happened to them. They have come into a living way with the Lord. Now, that is the aspect we talked about in verse two.

Now we see the Holy Spirit's work in renewing, reviving, keeping alive and fresh and vital. Don't you think we need this too? Oh, my word. I mean, how can brethren dwell together in unity when we are all getting jaded and faded and weary together? Doesn't it become an awful burden? I hear someone open their big mouth, and I know exactly what they are going to say. I know the very phrases they are going to use.

You know the kind of thing, brother So-and-So will get up at 11 o'clock and open the meeting. Oh, the times I have heard about, especially in the dear Brethren assemblies. They say, "Well, we are led of the Lord, but we know brother So-and-So will open the meeting at 11 o'clock every Sunday, and brother So-and-So, another brother, will close the meeting at 12 o'clock. Led by the Spirit, of course." But I mean, it is always the same. It was wonderful in the day, in the heyday of the moving of the Holy Spirit. It was all alive! It was wonderful! But now we have got used to each other.

My dear friends, if we are all butterflies moving on from place to place, we can escape this. See if I come into this company, and I listen to everybody, I would say, "Oh! It is wonderful! Such phrases, such language, such intimacy, such directness." When I have been here ten years, I almost know myself what everyone will say. I could say, "Shut up, brother So-and-So, I will say it for you." I have no doubt that some would say it to me, "Oh, shut up, brother, we can say it for you. We know you so well. We know you inside out. We know almost how you will put it."

Now, I say that this becomes a source of irritation after a while. It sure does. It becomes a source of irritation after a while because we think, "Oh, why doesn't So-and-So shut up? I have heard it all before. Why can't we have something fresh?"

That is the dew. That is why this whole matter is connected with brethren dwelling together in unity. If you and I want to stay together in unity, the dead leaves have to go. The dead wood has to be cut out. All the time it has got to be kept anew. Of course, we shall sometimes say the same thing, but it is in life. There is a vast difference when it is in life and when it is in death, when it is just a mumbo jumbo, or whether it is just a little phrase or two that we have used for years that just comes out without hardly thinking and it is in life. It is the worship of an adoring heart.

Quiet, Hidden, Gentle, Consistent

This, I say, is a very important matter. This is the Holy Spirit's work, renewing us. Re-*newing* us. Keeping us new all the time, not novel, but renewing us, reviving us, keeping us alive and fresh and vital. It is a quiet work. It is not dramatic. It is quiet. It is gentle. This work of the Holy Spirit is a very gentle work.

You know when the Holy Spirit anoints us, He really does sometimes nearly knock us out. Dennis, whenever he writes to me, always signs at the end of the letter: "May God bless you as much as you can take and not knock you out." I mean, although it is in Dennis's way of fun, it is so true! When the Holy Spirit really comes upon a person, there are times when you can burst! I have known brothers who have said, "No more Lord, no more. I cannot take anymore." Now, maybe you have never had an experience like that. Well, you have still got it to come. Do not give up. He may come to any of you, but the fact of the matter is this: that it is dynamic.

Now, this other work of the Holy Spirit is very gentle. There is no one here who has ever heard the dew fall. You have never heard, Plop! "Ah! The dew! Did you hear it? It fell a moment ago." You have never heard the rushing sound of wind and thought, "The dew is here! Praise the Lord!" No, no, it is so gentle, so hidden in action, no one sees the dew form. You can stand out in the open and you will not see it. It is hidden in action. One moment it is not there, the next moment it is there.

This is the work of the Holy Spirit in renewing and quickening and keeping in life. It is inward and hidden so often in its operation, always known in its fruit. Do not let anyone misunderstand me on this matter, that this is so hidden that you never see it in a life. You can tell a life that has the dew of heaven upon it because the dew always has something to do with the ripening of fruit in Israel and you see it in a person's life. They may be in the battle, they may be in the conflict, they may be in the storm, but there is fruit in that life, which is ripening by the inward, gentle, consistent, regular, continuous work of the Holy Spirit.

Daily Renewing by the Holy Spirit

Now, let us go on and look into the Scripture a little more together. Let us underline this vital necessity of being renewed daily. We will start in the New Testament, then we will go to the Old Testament. Let us take II Corinthians 4:16–18. Oh, these are such well known words. Now, do not shut off, but listen very carefully to these well-known words: "Wherefore we faint not." Did you hear that you who are fainting? "Wherefore we faint not. But though our outward man is decaying," Aha dear ones, those who are extreme charismatics amongst us, will you please note that "though our outward man is decaying." We cannot stop our teeth falling out, our hair falling out, our eyesight failing. Sometimes the Lord comes in and touches it, but we are decaying.

For many people, this could be a source of very real discouragement. I have no doubt that some who are beginning to get a little older, especially as you get in your late 20s and early 30s, you begin to feel a kind of discouragement coming that there is a relentless work of decay going on in your body. And therefore, you become weary, and you become discouraged, and you feel you do not really want to look too much in the mirror, you know, and all the rest of it. But the Bible says this, "Wherefore we faint not. But though our outward man is decaying, yet our inward man is being renewed day by day."

Then it goes on, "For our light affliction, which is for a moment, worketh for us, more and more exceedingly an eternal weight of glory, while we look not at the things which are seen, but at the things which are not seen, for the things which are seen are temporal, but the things which are not seen are eternal." Now, the accent of this wonderful little passage is on this: "our inward man is being renewed, day by day." Day by day a renewal, daily renewal—dew of heaven—quiet, gentle, hidden in operation, life-giving, continuous. What a wonderful word!

Look again, at Titus 3:5, "Not by works done in righteousness, which we did ourselves, but according to His mercy, he saved us through the washing of regeneration, and the renewing of the Holy Spirit." Through the washing of regeneration and the renewing. It is not enough to be born again. It is not enough just to be born again, dear child of God. To be born again is the most wonderful thing in the world, but you must also be renewed by the Holy Spirit. This is a continual, consistent, regular ministry of the Spirit to us, keeping us alive. Oh, that we knew it! Do we have to go from conference to conference? From prayer and Bible week to prayer and Bible week? Shall we go from high point to high point sort of, "Oh, I had a marvellous time; now I feel ready for the next two months." We go on for two months, then we start to go down, the old motor starts to run down, and we think, "Oh God, if only You will bring brother So-and-So, or So-and-So back. May he lay hands upon me, may something happen and I will get a new steam!"

You know me well enough to know that I believe in a real experience of the Holy Spirit, and not just one. There is a real initial experience, but there are many experiences of the Holy Spirit. However, there is a quiet, inward, consistent, continuous ministry of the Holy Spirit. If you do not know that, then your life will be a whole strain. You will just go up and then slowly down. Then up. Then down. It will be such a strain. You and I, we need to know, not only those great incomings of the Holy Spirit, those anointings of the Holy Spirit, we need to also know the being renewed by the Holy Spirit.

Renewed — Springs of Living Water

Let us go on and look at John 4:14. Although it is not in quite the same vein, it has, I think, some little commentary on this. Listen to these words of our Lord Jesus to the Samaritan woman, "But whosoever drinketh of the water that I shall give him shall never thirst; but the water that I shall give him shall become in him a well of water springing up unto eternal life."

Here is used the thought of a spring, not just a well where the water gathers. In the East you have (I suppose we have had it here in this country too, before we had piped water), you have wells where water seeps in and you let a bucket down and take it out. You also have the kind of thing which is a spring. It bubbles up and bubbles down. It is fresh all the time.

Now, this that the Lord gives to you is not a well that you have to continually go with bucket down and pull up a bucket full of living water and have a drink. This is something that springs up and down. It is not always in the same strength. This is where some people make their great mistake, you see, because they think all the time that everything should be absolutely level all the way through. But no. There are winters to be gone through, as well as springs and summers. Spiritual winters, when there is a time of contraction, where the frost does its hard work in us, where all kinds of things drop off and seem to be dead and are left behind. Then there comes a new spring and a new summer. There is a further expansion, a greater growth. This is a spiritual law. It is so with this wonderful spring of water springing up. Sometimes it springs right up and sometimes it drops, but it is always there. What a wonderful thought of renewing.

Have you found the spring within you? It is the Lord. Have you found the Holy Spirit within you as the spring springing up unto eternal life? It goes right back to this Psalm: "Like the dew of Hermon that cometh down upon the mountains of Zion. There the Lord commanded the blessing, even life for evermore." Eternal life, springing up unto life eternal. Tremendous!

Renewing the Mind

Or again, look at Colossians 3:10: "And have put on the new man, that is being renewed unto knowledge." You put on the new man which is being renewed unto knowledge. Now, in the New American Standard Bible it says, "You have put on the new self who is being renewed to a true knowledge." Being renewed to a true knowledge.

Now, will you notice therefore, that this being renewed has something to do with the mind. It has something to do with the mind. Look at Romans 12:2. You will see it much more clearly there. "And be not fashioned according to this world: but be ye transformed by the renewing of your mind, that ye may prove what is the good and acceptable and perfect will of God."

A brother said to me the other day that in his studies he had found that this word "acceptable" would be much better rendered "suitable." I think that is beautiful. Something that is suitable to you, the good and suitable and perfect will of God. How can anyone prove what is the good and suitable and perfect will of God for them, unless they have been delivered from the fashion of this world and transformed by the renewing of their mind?

Now, this is where we come to this whole matter of weariness and jadedness. It is all in our mind. If you and I live according to the old mind and the old man and the old ways and the fashion of this world, when we come into the new, we are all the time like fish out of water. We need to be transformed by the renewing of our mind. When truth breaks into a person, when they come to a true knowledge, each successive step, each further illumination, enlightenment, it is as if they are freed from something and brought into a new way with the Lord.

"Transformed by the renewing of your mind." It is in our mind, isn't it, that so much of the problem is. Don't you think so? I do. I know that my mind is the thing that makes me tired. I find that my mind is all the time arguing, discussing, telling me what is right. It is the real tree of the knowledge of good and evil, always weighing up this and weighing up that and saying, "This is better than that," and "do this," and "this is the logical thing to do." I get so tired because so often my mind is in conflict with the mind of God. He says, "Do this" and I think, "Oh, don't be silly. I mean, if I do that it will be the end of me." Or, "Go this way" and I say, "No, it cannot be right. My instinct of self-preservation tells me I cannot do that. It is too much, Lord. Good and suitable? Your will, good and suitable and perfect? No, no, no. I think I have got a better idea of it, Lord, than You. I know what is good for me and suitable for me and perfect for me." Then we get very, very distant, as far as the Lord is concerned. We are left as it were to our own ways, our own resources, our own energies, our own mind, and all the rest of it. It is an important point. We need to be transformed by the renewing of our mind.

Now, this dew is the renewing of our mind, you see. Look back to the day you were converted. In that moment you were, for the first time, in newness. You had a new mind. You had new thoughts. Oh, you were only just beginning. Do you remember that for the first time you began to trust the Lord, and the joy of trusting the Lord? Do you remember that when you did something that your old mind said, "Don't be stupid," but your new mind in the Lord said, "Yes, yes, yes, that is the mind of Christ," you did it, and you found such blessing, and such life? You were overjoyed. Your heart bubbled over. You did not know who you could tell quickly enough about what the Lord meant to you. You were transformed by the renewing of your mind. Unfortunately, as we go on, oh dear, we fall back from that. We start to do what comes naturally, or many other things. The ways of this world take over. Then we become somehow or other faded and weary, and all the time tired and disgruntled, and empty and discontented, and so it goes on and on.

In Ephesians 4:23–24, you have got the same thing again: "And that ye be renewed in the spirit of your mind, and put on the new man, that after God hath been created in righteousness and holiness of truth." That ye be renewed in the spirit of your mind.

Our minds are very important. Some believers tell us we should not use our minds. They tell us the mind spells death. Well, there is an old mind that does spell death, but there is a very important emphasis in the Word of God on the renewing of our mind. When we have a renewed mind, it is as if for the first time, we see it to be logical to trust the Lord. We see suddenly that it is the most rational thing in the whole world to do the will of God because if you do the will of God, all the provision of God is yours, all the protection of God is yours, all the resources of God are yours, all the energy of God is yours. The very resurrection power of Christ is yours if you do the will of God. This is what we find again and again. We do the impossible when we trust the Lord, and we come out with more life, more joy, and more fullness than we ever had when we went in.

However, look at these other people who draw back. They say they can't do this, they can't do that. It would kill them to do this, this is too much for them. Oh, they can't, so they draw back, draw back, draw back. What happens? Within six months, they are dead—dead, dry branches, withered and jaded. The more they draw back, the less life they have. The less joy they have. The less fullness they have. Isn't it interesting? Get out of the will of God, and there is no provision. You are left to yourself. In the will of God, you have got everything. Dew of heaven.

This renewing is of the utmost importance. It is absolutely necessary if we are to go on to the Lord's end. Do you want to go on to the Lord's end? I do. I would love to go on right to the Lord's end. Now, if you are going to go on to the Lord's end and I am going to go on to the Lord's end, this matter of the dew of heaven is of the utmost importance. We have got to know the renewing of the Lord, not just a month here and a month there, but we have got to know it continuously.

Renewed as the Eagle

Now look at the Old Testament and you find it just as exciting in the Old Testament. Look at Psalm 103:5. This is a wonderful Psalm, which I suppose everybody here knows pretty well, "Who satisfieth thy desire with good things, So that thy youth is renewed like the eagle." Now, this does not seem to quite tie up with decaying. Oh, yes, it does. I know people who have not got their own teeth, but they have got a good deal more energy than some of the young people here. (That is putting it crudely.) Decay is doing its work, but they have got energy. Their youth is renewed as the eagle. They have got stamina. To put it again very crudely, they have got spiritual guts. They have got what it takes to go through. Why? Because they have got an experience of this gentle, hidden, quiet ministry of the Holy Spirit, renewing, renewing, renewing. Their youth is renewed deeply on the inside. They are always young.

It is lovely to meet young people. It is always a blessing, isn't it, when someone comes in, dances in full of life, full of gaiety? Well, it is lovely when we do not get old spiritually, you know, all sorts of arthritis and rheumatism. But so many of us, oh my goodness, we have only got to be five, six years old in the Lord and we are real rheumatics in bath chairs, you know, with ear trumpets. We do not anymore hear the word of the Lord. You know, "What's He saying?" The Lord has to bawl at us before we even get a single word from heaven. We have lost it. We are old; we are no longer young. We are not those who have got a keen hearing, keen sight, keen senses full of life, limbs full of life.

Oh, that God could renew our youth like the eagle. The eagle is an extraordinary bird. In a few moments it can soar almost a mile into the air. I have seen eagles in Sinai and in Galilee. On one occasion when we stopped, there was one great big creature on the road in front of us; it was actually a vulture, the most ungainly thing you have ever seen. It had a six-foot wingspan, dancing about like a dance of death on the road until it lifted up and within moments it was a speck above us with four others. Youth like the eagle, strength, soaring to the heavens.

Now, some people want to have an experience that will catapult them like Cape Kennedy out into outer space spiritually you know, sort of "VOOM" and they are off. You will never get that way by spiritual experience, there is a need of an anointing. Dear child of God, there is also this need of the continuous consistent ministry of the Holy Spirit.

Now, let us just look at a few more scriptures here. Look at Psalm 51. Have you ever prayed like this? Psalm 51:10: "Create in me a clean heart, O God; And renew a right spirit within me." Sometimes, when we have fallen away from the Lord we need to pray "renew a right spirit within me." Now, in both these instances, Psalm 103 and Psalm 51, the word is a very simple word in Hebrew that just means to "make new or to renew." It is as simple as that.

I have thought also of Psalm 23:3. You all know it so well you never think about it. "He restoreth my soul." Does the Lord ever restore your soul? What does that imply? That there are times when our soul is drained, but He restores it. Now, if we keep in the way of God, we are going to have battles. We are going to have conflicts. There are going to be terrible pressures, but thank God, there is also the restoring of our soul. We will be renewed if we keep within the will of God, but if we get out of it, nothing.

Now, I want you also to look at Isaiah 40. Here we come nearest, I think, to the heart of this whole matter in the Bible of renewing. Psalm 40:27–31: "Why sayest thou, O Jacob, and speakest, O Israel, My way is hid from the Lord, and the justice due to me is passed away from my God? Hast thou not known? hast thou not heard? The everlasting God, Jehovah, the Creator of the ends of the earth, fainteth not, neither is weary; there is no searching of his understanding. He giveth power to the faint; and to him that hath no might he increaseth strength."

Now, what a wonderful promise that is: He never faints, and He is never weary, and there is no searching of His understanding. To those who are faint He gives power and to those who have no might He increaseth strength. Then go on: "Even the youth shall faint and be weary, and the young men shall utterly fall: but they that wait for the Lord shall renew their strength; they shall mount up with wings as eagles; they shall run, and not be weary; they shall walk, and not faint."

It is interesting, isn't it? The promise is, first, like eagles. If you cannot manage that, you will run and not be weary. If you cannot manage that, you will walk and not faint. At least you will not faint! Isn't that a wonderful promise? It is far more wonderful than perhaps we realise.

To Exchange their Strength

Years and years ago in Egypt, I remember one of those dear old missionaries saying to me about this word in Arabic, in the classical Arabic that she had in her Old Testament. She said, "You know, the word is not 'they shall renew their strength,' but 'they shall exchange their strength,'" and she said, "I think it has a real connection with the Hebrew." Now, of course, old Arabic and Hebrew are reasonably close together, but I have never ever looked it up until today. I was tremendously excited when looking at this word "renew." I found that it was not the simple word we have in Hebrew, "to make new, to be renewed, to renew," but it was the word, listen very carefully to it, it is this word ḥālap̄:[1] "to substitute, to cause to succeed, to change for the better, to renew."

Listen to these marvellous instances of its use, if you want to follow you can do it. You could well go and really study them on your knees. Genesis 35:2: "Then Jacob said unto his household, and to all that were with him, Put away the foreign gods that are among you, and purify yourselves, and change your garments." The word "change your garments," is the same Hebrew word ḥālap̄. Change your garments, get rid of them, put new ones on. So, that dear old missionary was probably right. Exchange your garments, change them, not just renew, but change. How wonderful!

Now, there is another wonderful word, Genesis 31:7: "And your father hath deceived me, and changed my wages ten times." It is the same word—changed my wages ten times. He that waiteth on the Lord shall change his strength. Now, I think that is far better than being renewed. It means that somehow, He will substitute His strength for my weakness. What I call strength, He will take it away, and He will give me His own.

---

1 The word in Hebrew is ḥālap̄ Strong's H2498

Or again, you have got it in a very well-known passage, Psalm 102:26. (You probably all know this because it is quoted in Hebrews.) "They shall perish [that is the heavens], but thou shalt endure; Yea, all of them shall wax old like a garment; As a vesture shalt thou change them, and they shall be changed." Here is the same Hebrew word again. Now isn't that exciting? I do not know if it does anything for you, but it does a lot for me. What it means is that this waiting upon the Lord means that in the most marvellous way His strength becomes mine. He substitutes His energies for mine, His resources for mine, His strength for mine, His wisdom for mine. He gives Himself.

The Pressure of the Conflict

There is no doubt that if the purpose of God of brethren dwelling together in unity is to be fulfilled, there will ensue very great conflict and very great battle. There will be unrelenting pressure upon any of those who are going to give themselves to the realisation of the purpose of God. That is obvious, isn't it? The building up of the body of Christ, the completion of the house of God, the preparation of the bride must and will involve us in not only violent assaults and battles, but a continual pressure upon us wearing us out by persistent, uninterrupted pressure.

Listen to me. Many servants of the Lord, and when I say servants, I do not mean people like myself only, who sort of travel around preaching, I mean all of you who are really given to the Lord, to do the will of God, whether in jobs or whatever, many servants of the Lord, good soldiers of Jesus Christ, who would never give way under ferocious attack and onslaught, collapse through weariness. Just weariness. We all know it, at the natural level a person gets weary and jaded, they become discouraged and depressed. Then all kinds of dark ideas begin to come and before long, you collapse. You give up. You draw back.

Now, if the enemy came with a violent attack upon you, and you knew it was the enemy, you would stand it. You would take the Lord, you would endure the storm, and you would come right through. However, when it is all the little nagging things like children crying all night, or suddenly one child after another gets measles, or somehow or other at work another load is put upon you, someone gets the sack, or someone walks out, and a whole great load comes on you—all these little things. Do you think it is coincidence? Do you really think it is coincidence if you are involved in a tremendous battle for the completion of the house of God? I don't.

If there is an enemy, and there is, if there is a satanic hierarchy, and there is, if there is a kind of spiritual headquarters planning satanic strategy, and there is, then it seems to be most reasonable to believe that if they know we are involved in something to do with the completion of the purpose of God, every single thing about us is taken into account. This one will be brought down, not by the big things (because we recognise them) but by the little tiny things. Then this one, and that one, and the other one, and the other one, until we hardly know what has happened, but there are casualties all over the place. There is just a general atmosphere of weariness and tiredness.

Wait on the Lord

This is why the matter of renewing is so important. It is a daily matter. It has to do with the mind. It comes through the Holy Spirit. It always results in dependence upon the Lord. You see, people ask me straightaway, "Then how does this happen?" I tell you, by waiting upon the Lord. That is the one thing for which many of us find no time. "I cannot wait upon the Lord; I have no time! Already I have had to cut this out and cut that out and cut the other out, do you think I can also wait?"

But you know, five minutes waiting upon the Lord will probably mean five hours of renewing. Just to be still. It is the most essential thing in the whole world, but we do not see it, nor does the enemy let us. He knows it is far too valuable to let anybody see that. So he says, "You can't do it; you can't do it. Out of bed. Go on, get on with it. Quick! Out!" You read the Scripture—bluh, bluh, bluh, bluh, bluh—one verse—that's your quiet time. Out. Down the road. Off to work. Then we are so tired and we say, "Oh, dear, dear, dear; I can't face that Bible study tonight. Prayer? I could not face it. That job I was going to do? No, no. Visit So-and-So? I can't do that. I am tired." So, of course, next day, we say, "It is no good Lord. You know how tired I am. I know You understand. I won't wait upon You."

Now the Lord does understand. He does not want you to wait upon Him in a state like that. "Well, My dear child, I understand entirely. But don't you understand? It is your own welfare. If you could only see that to wait on Me for a few minutes would bring a whole different attitude. You could be renewed in mind.

You would understand that it is not for Me, it is for you. You are spiting yourself, not Me."

You see the Lord wants the dew of heaven to come upon us. That is His desire. But we often are so silly, that we have no time for the quiet working of the Lord. Now, if you and I could learn this one little lesson, it would transform many of us. I believe it would transform all of us, for it is really a matter of great importance.

As we have said, often the enemy gets advantage in this question of our unity, not by the great frontal attacks, but by reducing us to a weary, heavy, sluggish, faded state. Then when that happens, we are robbed of joy, of peace, and we are paralysed as far as contributing goes, as far as functioning goes. Even the discharging of our responsibilities given us of God we find we cannot do. Many times we drop out, sometimes without any warning, and the effect is precisely what the enemy intended: greater strain is put on the others. They in turn become weary—more weary, more tired and so it goes on until the enemy has knocked us all out, not by a great frontal onslaught, but by simple pressure. The Scripture talks about the wearing out of the saints in the latter days. I do not think we are yet there, but my dear friends if we are feeling it now, what is it going to be like in another ten years? It also speaks about the love of the many waxing cold, listen, because iniquity is multiplied. Now what does that mean? Unless it means that there is so much iniquity, that the very atmosphere is filled with antagonism, and it wears out the saints.

Now, if we know these things from the Word, the most important thing for us is to wake up to the fact that this is a spiritual thing. It is not just a natural thing. I am all for when a person is genuinely tired, it is a good thing just to go to bed. If you are really that dog-tired, as sometimes happens, it is best not just to try and be the great hero and the champion, but just to give in and go to bed. However, it is an altogether different thing when we start cutting one thing out, then the next, then the next, then the next. It is the thin end of the wedge. Before we know where we are, what happens in our spiritual life? We are not more alive. We are not more joyful. We have not more peace. We have less and less and less. We cut out more and more and more. We have less time, less joy, less peace, and less life.

What is the answer then to the whole thing? We must never forget that when you remain within the will of God, within that position, there is a provision of renewing. If God has given you a tough job to do, God will see that you know the dew of heaven. It is there for you. Therefore, you have just to find it, if you will only give time, wait on the Lord and wait for the Lord. It is as simple as that. Outside of His will, there is only greater weariness and emptiness and alienation.

So, we come to the end of this Psalm. We need to remember those words which are a commentary on what I have said this evening: "Trust in the Lord with all thine heart, and lean not upon thy own understanding. In all thy ways acknowledge Him, and He will direct thy paths." Proverbs 3:5,6. We lean upon our own understanding often in so many things, not realizing that it is the enemy.

Now, what has God promised? He says this: "For there, the Lord commanded the blessing, even life forevermore." Isn't that marvellous? It is a commanded blessing. What is the commanded blessing? Eternal life. Oh, that is what I want. So, this renewing is commanded by the Lord Himself. Life eternal.

It reminds me of that wonderful Scripture, that if we sow to the spirit, we shall of the spirit reap life eternal. If we sow to the flesh, we shall of the flesh reap corruption unto death. This is a matter of the mind. Follow the way of the world, the fashion of the world—that does not just mean clothes, the fashion of the world means the whole outlook of the world, the way the world sees things, the worldly outlook—follow it and it leads to death. Follow the mind of the Spirit and it leads to life.

This is a marvellous Psalm, this little Psalm 133. It seems to me that this last little phase, "For there the Lord commanded the blessing, even life forevermore," actually is a conclusion to the whole Psalm, going right back to brethren dwelling together in unity. It is as if the Lord is saying, "Where brethren dwell together in unity, there the Lord, I, have commanded the blessing, even life forevermore. Where brethren know the precious oil upon the head, running down upon the beard, down to the hem of the garment, there I have commanded the blessing, even life forevermore. Where they know this quiet, continuous ministry of the Holy Spirit, renewing, quickening, empowering, keeping in life, there I have commanded the blessing, even life forevermore."

In the end, that is what this weary world in all its sin and emptiness is looking for. Not meetings, not words, not hymns, not great songs, and all the rest of it. What the world is looking for is life. When it sees in other human beings, lives that have been changed by the power of God and are alive, who know the Lord, who have joy in their hearts, who have peace in their hearts, then I believe the world begins to take note, don't you? May God make us like that. It does not mean we do not have troubles, my word we shall. It does not mean we will not have problems; we shall. But then we have provision. If there are going to be problems, there is also provision. Let us find the provision. Don't let us go back in this year of '78, but let us go forward strongly, firmly into all that the Lord has for us. He will be with us.

Shall we pray?

Father, we just spread this out before Thee. Oh, Lord, there is not one of us in this room that does not need renewing. We feel it, Lord, so often in our hearts in these days of pressure, days of relentless wearing out of Thy children by the powers of darkness. Lord, we pray that Thou would help us. Help us to be more open, as it were, to one another Lord, when these things happen in our circumstance, to ask for prayer to share with one another that we may be covered. Lord, we want to be kept in life, not just one or two of us, but all of us, Lord. We want to be people who know the renewing of that dew of heaven. So that we are kept alive, so that there is fruit Lord, ripening for Thee. Oh, Father, so that there is fragrance for others, shade for others. Lord, Thou alone canst do this. Teach us to wait for Thee and wait upon Thee, so that we may change our strength, we may mount up with wings as eagles, run and not be weary, walk and not faint. Lord, then we commit this into Thy hands, these studies upon this little Psalm 133. Wilt Thou, Lord, engrave it upon our hearts and in our life together as Thy people. We ask it in the name of our Lord Jesus. Amen.

Reigning with Christ

Spiritual Character

Talks with Leaders

The Battle of the Ages

The Eternal Purpose of God

The Glory of Thy People Israel

The Gospel of the Kingdom

The Importance of Covering

The Last Days and God's Priorities

The Prize

The Relevance of Biblical Prophecy

The Silent Years

The Supremacy of Jesus

The Uniqueness of Israel

The Way to the Eternal Purpose of God

They Shall Mount up with Wings

Thine Is the Power

Thou Art Mine

Through the Bible with Lance Lambert: Genesis - Deuteronomy

Till the Day Dawns

Unity : Behold How Good and How Pleasant
- Ministries from Psalm 133

Warring the Good Warfare

What Is God Doing?: Lessons from Church History

The Relevance of Biblical Prophecy

And we have the word of prophecy made more sure; whereunto ye do well that ye take heed, as unto a lamp shining in a dark place, until the day dawn, and the day-star arise in your hearts
II Peter 1:19

"A lamp shining in a dark place ..." Thank God for the Word, but thank God for the prophetic word, which is like a lamp shining in a squalid place, that can give us light so that we can read the chart, so that we can see the map, so that we can see where we're going, so we can understand where we have arrived and at what point we are on the journey. (p. 32)

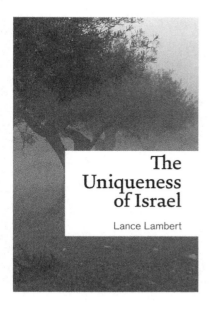

The
Uniqueness
of Israel

Lance Lambert

The Uniqueness of Israel

Woven into the fabric of Jewish existence there is an undeniable uniqueness. There is bitter controversy over the subject of Israel, but time itself will establish the truth about this nation's place in God's plan. For Lance Lambert, the Lord Jesus is the key that unlocks Jewish history He is the key not only to their fall, but also to their restoration. For in spite of the fact that they rejected Him, He has not rejected them.

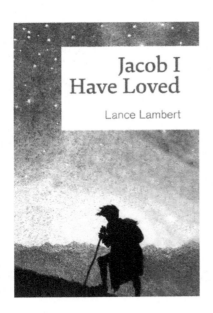

Jacob I Have Loved

Jacob I
Have Loved

Lance Lambert

Jacob I Have Loved

When God deals with us it is often in deeply mystifying ways. There is no greater example of how God shapes a person than through the remarkable story of Jacob. *Jacob I Have Loved* is far more than a mere biblical overview of the story of Jacob. It is an outstanding illustration of God's desire to utterly transform our fallen inner nature. Despite a twisted, deceiving, and sinful heart, Jacob nonetheless inherited God's richest blessings and became one of the patriarchs of our faith. Herein lies one of the Bible's great mysteries. The amazing truth is that Jacob's name has not been lost in the debris of human history, nor has it been forgotten, as have so many other names. Incredibly, it is forever linked with God. His story is an integral part of the history of divine redemption. This book is about the power of God to transform a human life.

Through the Bible with Lance Lambert: Ezra, Nehemiah, Esther

"The Bible is not a history book. History is only found in the Scripture when it has something to teach us." (page 62)

Recovery. This key theme throughout the entire timeline of Ezra to Esther gives us a clear vision of the Lord's goal with His people. From the building of Jerusalem and its surrounding walls in Ezra and Nehemiah to the fixing of the irreversible decree of the annihilation of Jews in Esther, the Lord is constantly using His people for recovery. In this book of the series, "Through the Bible with Lance Lambert," we find an in depth analysis of Ezra, Nehemiah, and Esther, tracing the working of the Lord throughout history.

Made in the USA
Las Vegas, NV
17 June 2022

50388744R00079